THE SYSTEM OF OBJECTS

THE SYSTEM OF OBJECTS

Jean Baudrillard

Translated by James Benedict

VERSO

London • New York

First published by Verso 1996
This edition published by Verso 2005
Translation © James Benedict 1996, 2005
First published as *Le système des objets*
© Editions Gallimard 1968

Published with the financial assistance of the French Ministry of Culture

10

Verso
UK: 6 Meard Street, London W1F 0EG
USA: 20 Jay Street, Suite 1010, Brooklyn, NY 11201
www.versobooks.com

Verso is the imprint of New Left Books

ISBN 1-84467-053-8
ISBN 978-1-84467-053-6

British Library Cataloguing in Publication Data
A catalogue record for this book is available from the British Library

Library of Congress Cataloging-in-Publication Data
A catalog record for this book is available from the Library of Congress

Typeset in Garamond by Hewer Text UK Ltd
Printed and bound by CPI Group (UK) Ltd, Croydon, CR0 4YY

Contents

Translator's Acknowledgements

For her unstinting help with this translation, I must yet again offer my heartfelt gratitude to M.N. Many many thanks as well to Malcolm Imrie and Jane Hindle, my editors at Verso.

Introduction

Could we classify the luxuriant growth of objects as we do a flora or fauna, complete with tropical and glacial species, sudden mutations, and varieties threatened by extinction? Our urban civilization is witness to an ever-accelerating procession of generations of products, appliances and gadgets by comparison with which mankind appears to be a remarkably stable species. This pullulation of objects is no odder, when we come to think about it, than that to be observed in countless natural species. Species which man has successfully inventoried. And in the period when he began to do this systematically he was also able to draw up, in the *Encyclopédie*, an exhaustive catalogue of the practical and technical objects that surrounded him. Since then, however, that balance has been lost: everyday objects (we are not concerned here with machines) proliferate, needs multiply, production speeds up the life-span of such objects – yet we lack the vocabulary to name them all. How can we hope to classify a world of objects that changes before our eyes and arrive at an adequate system of description? There are almost as many criteria of classification as there are objects themselves: the size of the object; its degree of functionality (i.e. the object's relationship to its own objective function); the gestures associated with it (are they rich or impoverished? traditional or not?); its form; its duration; the time of day at which it appears (more or less intermittent presence, and how conscious one is of it); the material that it transforms (obvious in the case of a coffee grinder, less so in those of a mirror, a radio, or a car – though every object transforms something); the degree of exclusiveness or sociability attendant upon its use (is it for private, family, public or general use?); and so on. Indeed all such means of categorization may seem – when they are applied to an ensemble, such as the set of objects, that is undergoing continual mutation and expansion – barely less contingent than the order of the letters of the alphabet. The catalogue of the Manufacture d'Armes de Saint-Etienne proposes, if not structures, then at least subdivisions, but it takes into account only objects defined according to function: each object corresponds to an operation, often a tiny or heteroclite operation, but nowhere is any *system* of meanings even touched upon.[1] At a much higher level, the simultaneously formal, functional and structural analysis which Siegfried Giedion offers us – a kind of epic history of the technical object[2] – notes the changes in social structure associated with technical development, but scarcely addresses such questions as how objects are experienced, what needs other than functional ones they answer, what mental structures are interwoven with – and contradict – their functional structures, or what cultural, infracultural or transcultural system underpins their directly experienced everydayness. These are the questions we shall be asking here. We shall not, therefore, be concerning ourselves with objects as defined by their functions or by the categories into which they might be subdivided for analytic purposes, but instead with the processes whereby people relate to them and with the systems of human behaviour and relationships that result therefrom.

The study of this 'spoken' system of objects – that is, the study of the more or less consistent system of meanings that objects institute – always presupposes a plane distinct from this 'spoken'

1. The catalogue itself, however – its actual existence – is rich in meaning: its exhaustive nomenclatural aims have the resounding cultural implication that access to objects may be obtained only via the pages of a catalogue which may be leafed through 'for the pleasure of it', as one might a great manual, a book of tales, a menu. . . .

2. *Mechanization Takes Command* (New York: Oxford University Press, 1948).

system, a more strictly structured plane, a structural plane transcending even the functional account of objects. This plane is the technological one.

The technological plane is an abstraction: in ordinary life we are practically unconscious of the technological reality of objects. Yet this abstraction is profoundly real: it is what governs all radical transformations of our environment. It is even – and I do not mean this in any paradoxical sense – the most concrete aspect of the object, for technological development is synonymous with objective structural evolution. In the strictest sense, what happens to the object in the technological sphere is *essential*, whereas what happens to it in the psychological or sociological sphere of needs and practices is *inessential*. The discourse of psychology or sociology continually refers us to the object as apprehended at a more consistent level, a level unrelated to any individual or collective discourse, namely the supposed level of *technological* language. It is starting from this language, from this consistency of the technical model, that we can reach an understanding of what happens to objects by virtue of their being produced and consumed, possessed and personalized.

It is imperative, therefore, to get a clear picture from the outset of the rationality of the object – a clear picture, that is, of the objective technological structure involved. Take, for example, Gilbert Simondon's account of the petrol engine:

> In today's engines each important part is so closely associated with the others by reciprocal exchanges of energy that it cannot undergo any essential variation whatsoever. . . . The form of the cylinder head, the metal of which it is manufactured, works in combination with all the other elements of the cycle to produce a particular temperature in the electrodes of the sparking-plug; this temperature in turn affects the characteristics of the ignition and of the cycle as a whole.
>
> Modern engines are concrete, whereas earlier ones were abstract. In the older version, each component intervened at a specific stage of the cycle and was then supposed to have no

further impact on the others; motor parts were rather like people, each doing their job without ever getting acquainted with their co-workers. . . . The technical object may thus be said to have a primitive form, an abstract form, in which each theoretical and material unit is treated as an absolute needing to be set up as a closed system if it is to function properly. Such a situation presents a set of problems of integration that have to be resolved. . . . This is the point at which specific structures emerge which, relative to each component, one might call defence mechanisms: for instance, the cylinder head of the internal-combustion heat engine starts to bristle with cooling fins. These were at first simply an extraneous element, as it were, added to the cylinder and the cylinder head for the sole purpose of cooling. In more recent engines, however, these fins have come to play a mechanical role as well by providing a ribbing that serves to inhibit the distortion of the cylinder head under the pressure of gases. . . . Now the two functions are no longer distinguishable; a unique structure has thus evolved, one which is not a compromise but a concomitance, a convergence. The ribbed cylinder head may now be made thinner, which allows for faster cooling. The bivalent fin/rib structure therefore fulfils the two formerly separate functions by means of a synthesis – and the result is far more satisfactory in both cases: it integrates the two functions and transcends them. . . . We may say, then, that the new structure is more concrete than the old and that it represents a genuine advance for the technical object, for the true technological problem is the need for a convergence of functions within a single structural feature, not the need for a compromise between conflicting requirements. Ultimately, this progression from abstract to concrete means that the technical object will tend towards the state of a system that is completely internally consistent and completely unified.[3]

3. Gilbert Simondon, *Du mode d'existence des objects techniques* (Paris: Aubier, 1958), pp. 25–6.

This analysis is invaluable, because it supplies us with the elements of a coherent system that is never directly experienced, never apprehended at the practical level. Technology gives us a rigorous account of objects in which functional antagonisms are dialectically resolved into larger structures. Every transition from a system to another, better-integrated system, every commutation within an already structured system, every functional synthesis, precipitates the emergence of a meaning, an objective pertinence that is independent of the individuals who are destined to put it into operation; we are in effect at the level of a language here, and, by analogy with linguistic phenomena, those simple technical elements – different from real objects – upon whose interplay technological evolution is founded might well be dubbed 'technemes'.

It is quite possible to envision a science of structural technology working at this level that would study the organization of such technemes into more complex technical objects. This science could be strictly applied, however, only to a limited number of areas, ranging from laboratory research to the massive technological products of the aeronautics, astronautics, shipbuilding, heavy-vehicle or heavy-machinery industries. These are precisely the areas where technical pressures maximize structural constraints, where the collective and impersonal nature of the product reduces the effects of fashion to a minimum. Whereas car makers must continually explore every conceivable variation in the form of their product, while meeting a very few basic technological requirements (water cooling, cylinder-based engine, etc.), aircraft manufacturers are obliged to produce concrete technical objects solely on the basis of simple functional imperatives (safety, speed, efficiency, and so on). Here technological development follows an almost pure course. So, if we want to account for the system of *everyday* objects, a structural technological analysis is clearly inadequate.

We may dream of arriving at an exhaustive description of technemes and their semantic relations that would cover the entire world of real objects, but this must inevitably remain just that – a dream. It is therefore tempting to deal with technemes just as Plato would have us deal, as true astronomers, with the stars: 'If we mean, then, to turn the soul's native intelligence to its proper use by a genuine study of astronomy, we shall proceed, as we do in geometry, by means of problems, and leave the starry heavens alone.'[4] Unfortunately, this impulse immediately runs into the directly experienced psychological and sociological reality of objects, a reality which, over and above objects' perceptible materiality, constitutes such a significant body of constraints that the integrity of the technological system is continually being modified and disturbed by it. It is this disturbance, and the way the rationality of objects comes to grips with the irrationality of needs, and the way this contradiction gives rise to a system of meanings that seeks to resolve it – it is these things that we are concerned with here, not technological models, even if the essential truth of these models provides the ground from which our direct experience of objects is continually emerging.

Each of our practical objects is related to one or more structural elements, but at the same time they are all in perpetual flight from technical structure towards their secondary meanings, from the technological system towards a cultural system. The everyday environment remains to a very great extent an 'abstract' system. For all their multiplicity, objects are generally isolated as to their function, and it is the user who is responsible, as his needs dictate, for their coexistence in a functional context, in a system which is not very economical, not very consistent, and indeed resembles the archaic structure of early petrol engines in that it comprises an assortment of partial functions that are often irrelevant or antagonistic to one another. The current trend, moreover, is by no means to rectify this inconsistency but, rather, to meet successive needs by introducing new objects. The result is that each object

4. *The Republic of Plato*, trans F.M. Cornford (New York and London: Oxford University Press, 1945 [1941]), Book VII, pp. 248–9.

added to the sum of objects may be adequate to its own function but work against the whole; it even happens that a new object will be adequate to its function while at the same time working against it.

Furthermore, inasmuch as an object's formal and technical connotations are added to a functional incoherence, it is the whole system of needs, socialized or unconscious, cultural or practical – in short, a whole inessential system, directly experienced – which surges back on to the essential technical order and threatens the objective status of the object itself.

To take an example: the most 'essential' and structural aspects of a coffee mill, and hence the most concretely objective things about it, are the electric motor, the electricity furnished by the power company, and the laws governing the production and transformation of energy; what is already less objective, because it depends on a particular person's need, is the mill's actual coffee-grinding function; and what is not objective in the slightest, and hence inessential, is whether it is green and rectangular or pink and trapezoid. A single structure, the electric motor, may be embodied in a variety of specific functions; functional differentiation is thus already a secondary consideration (and may eventually fall into the sheer incoherence of the completely useless object or 'gadget'[5]). A single function of an object may in turn become specific in a variety of forms – which brings us into that realm of 'personalization', of formal connotation, where the inessential holds sway. Indeed, the characteristic of the industrial object which distinguishes it from the craft object is that in the former the inessential is no longer left to the whims of individual demand and manufacture, but instead picked up and systematized by the production process, which today defines its aims by reference to what is

5. [*Translator's note*: French, in borrowing the English word 'gadget', lays far more stress than English-speakers generally do on the connotation for which a gadget is an object, such as a novelty item, with no function or use value. It is with this emphasis that the author uses the term here and throughout the present work; see in particular his discussion of gadgets and robots below.]

inessential (and by reference to the universal combinatorial system of fashion).[6]

This inextricable complexity is what makes for the fact that the conditions under which a technological sphere may become autonomous, and therefore the possibility of a structural analysis in the realm of objects, are not comparable to the situation with regard to language. Apart from pure technical objects, with which as subjects we never have anything to do, we shall see that the two levels of objective denotation and of connotation (whereby the object is cathected, commercialized and personalized, whereby it attains utility and enters into a cultural system) are not, under today's conditions of production and consumption, separable in the way that the levels of language [*langue*] and speech [*parole*] are separable in linguistics. The technological level simply does not have the sort of structural autonomy that would permit us to say that its equivalent of 'speech acts', namely the 'speaking' object, is no more important in an analysis of objects than speech acts are in an analysis of linguistic phenomena. Whereas a rolled *r* in contrast to a uvular *r* changes nothing so far as the linguistic system is concerned – in other words, the connoted meaning has absolutely no retroactive effect on the denoted structures – the connotation of an object may for its part bring great weight to bear upon technical structures, and alter them significantly. For technology, unlike language, does not constitute a stable system. Unlike monemes and phonemes, technemes are continually evolving. Now, the fact that the technological system is so closely implicated, by reason of its state of permanent revolution, in the very *time* of the practical objects that 'speak' it (much the same is true for language, but to a vastly lesser degree); the fact that this system has as its aims a mastery of the world and the satisfaction of needs – aims, that is to say, which are more concrete and less easily

6. The modalities of transition from essential to inessential are thus today themselves relatively systematic. This systematization of the inessential has its sociological and psychological aspects; it also has an ideological function of integration (see 'Models and Series' below).

dissociated from praxis than communication, which is the aim of language; and, lastly, the fact that technology depends strictly on the *social* conditions under which technological research is carried out, and hence on the global order of production and consumption, an external constraint which in no way applies to language – all this means that the system of objects, unlike the linguistic system, cannot be described *scientifically* unless it is treated *in the process* as the result of the continual intrusion of a system of practices into a system of techniques. It is thus not consistent technical structures but, rather, the ways in which practices affect techniques – or, more exactly, the ways in which techniques are checked by practices – that account for reality here. In sum, the description of the system of objects cannot be divorced from a critique of that system's practical ideology. At the technological level there is no contradiction: there is merely intention. But a human science must be a science both of intention and of whatever counters that intention. How is it that a consistent technological system is disseminated as an inconsistent practical system? How is the 'language' of objects 'spoken'? By what means does this 'speech' system (or this system which falls somewhere between language and speech) override the linguistic system? And finally, what is the location, not of the abstract consistency of the system of objects but, rather, of its directly experienced contradictions?[7]

7. On the basis of this distinction, it is nevertheless possible to posit a close affinity between the analysis of objects on the one hand and linguistics (or, more precisely, semiology) on the other. Thus what I refer to in the field of objects as marginal (or inessential) difference is analogous to the semiological notion of 'field of dispersal'. This field

is made up of the varieties in execution of a unit (of a phoneme, for instance) as long as these varieties do not result in an alteration in meaning (that is, as long as they do not become pertinent variations) . . .: in the food system, for instance, we can speak of the dispersal field of a dish, which will be established by the limits within which this dish's name still signifies, whatever 'frills' preparers may add. . . . The varieties which make up the dispersal field are called   *cont'd over/*

7. *cont'd/ combinative variants.* . . . [These] do not participate in commutations of meaning; they are not pertinent. . . . Combinative variants have long been considered as phenomena pertaining to speech: they certainly are very close to it, but are nowadays held to pertain to language, since they are 'compulsory'. (Roland Barthes, 'Eléments de sémiologie', *Communications*, no. 4 [November 1964], p. 128. English translation by Annette Lavers and Colin Smith: *Elements of Semiology* [London: Jonathan Cape, 1967], pp. 84–5 [here slightly modified].)

Barthes adds that this notion is destined to become a central one in semiology, because variations of this kind, though they are non-signifying at the denotative level, may again become significant at the level of connotation.

Clearly the analogy between combinative variation and marginal difference is a profound one: both involve the inessential, both are without pertinence, both depend on a combinatorial system and become meaningful at the level of connotation. There is an essential difference between them, however: combinative variation remains external to the semiological plane of denotation, whereas marginal difference is, precisely, never 'marginal'. For the technological plane does not designate – as language *qua* system [*langue*] does for language in general [*langage*] – a fixed methodological abstraction which reaches the real world only by virtue of connotations; rather, it designates an evolving structural framework which connotations (inessential differences) arrest, stereotype and cause to regress. Technology's structural dynamism is paralysed, at the level of objects, in the differential subjectivity of the cultural system, which itself then retroactively impinges on the organization of technology.

A. The functional system, or objective discourse

I Structures of Interior Design

The Traditional Environment

The arrangement of furniture offers a faithful image of the familial and social structures of a period. The typical bourgeois interior is patriarchal; its foundation is the dining-room/bedroom combination. Although it is diversified with respect to function, the furniture is highly integrated, centring around the sideboard or the bed in the middle of the room. There is a tendency to accumulate, to fill and close off the space. The emphasis is on unifunctionality, immovability, imposing presence and hierarchical labelling. Each room has a strictly defined role corresponding to one or another of the various functions of the family unit, and each ultimately refers to a view which conceives of the individual as a balanced assemblage of distinct faculties. The pieces of furniture confront one another, jostle one another, and implicate one another in a unity that is not so much spatial as moral in character. They are ranged about an axis which ensures a regular chronology of actions; thanks to this permanent symbolization, the family is always present to itself. Within this private space each piece of furniture in turn, and each room, internalizes its own particular function and takes on the symbolic dignity pertaining to it – then the whole house puts the finishing touch to this integration of interpersonal relationships within the semi-hermetic family group.

All this constitutes an organism whose structure is the patriarchal relationship founded on tradition and authority, and whose heart is the complex affective relationship that binds all the family members together. Such a family home is a specific space which takes little account of any objective decorative requirements, because the primary function of furniture and objects here is to personify human relationships, to fill the space that they share between them, and to be inhabited by a soul.[1] The real dimension they occupy is captive to the moral dimension which it is their job to signify. They have as little autonomy in this space as the various family members enjoy in society. Human beings and objects are indeed bound together in a collusion in which the objects take on a certain density, an emotional value – what might be called a 'presence'. What gives the houses of our childhood such depth and resonance in memory is clearly this complex structure of inter-iority, and the objects within it serve for us as boundary markers of the symbolic configuration known as home. The caesura between inside and outside, and their formal opposition, which falls under the social sign of property and the psychological sign of the immanence of the family, make this traditional space into a closed transcendence. In their anthropomorphism the objects that fur-nish it become household gods, spatial incarnations of the emo-tional bonds and the permanence of the family group. These gods enjoyed a gentle immortality until the advent of a modern generation which has cast them aside, dispersed them – even, on occasion, reinstated them in an up-to-date nostalgia for whatever is old. As often with gods, furniture too thus gets a second chance to exist, and passes from a naïve utility into a cultural baroque.

The dining-room/bedroom pattern – an arrangement of mo-vable property closely bound up with the house as immovable property – continues to be widely pitched by advertisers to a vast public. Department stores such as Lévitan and Galeries Barbès still titillate the collective taste with evocations of 'decorative' ensem-bles – despite the fact that contours are now 'stylized', despite the

1. They may also have taste and style – or not, as the case may be.

fact that decoration is out of favour. This furniture still sells, not because it is cheaper but because it embodies the official certainties of the group and enjoys the sanction of the bourgeoisie. A further reason is that such monumental furniture (sideboard, bed or wardrobe) and its arrangement echo the persistence of traditional family structures across broad social strata of modern society.

The Modern Object Liberated in Its Function

The style of furniture changes as the individual's relationships to family and society change. Corner divans and beds, coffee tables, shelving – a plethora of new elements are now supplanting the traditional range of furniture. The organization of space changes, too, as beds become day-beds and sideboards and wardrobes give way to built-in storage. Things fold and unfold, are concealed, appear only when needed. Naturally such innovations are not due to free experiment: for the most part the greater mobility, flexibility and convenience they afford are the result of an involuntary adaptation to a shortage of space – a case of necessity being the mother of invention. Whereas the old-fashioned dining-room was heavily freighted with moral convention, 'modern' interiors, in their ingeniousness, often give the impression of being mere functional expedients. Their 'absence of style' is in the first place an absence of room, and maximum functionality is a solution of last resort whose outcome is that the dwelling-place, though remaining closed to the outside, loses its internal organization. Such a restructuring of space and the objects in it, unaccompanied by any reconversion, must in the first instance be considered an impoverishment.

The modern set of furniture, serially produced, is thus apparently destructured yet not restructured, nothing having replaced the expressive power of the old symbolic order. There is progress, nevertheless: between the individual and these objects, which are now more supple in their uses and have ceased to exercise or symbolize moral constraint, there is a much more liberal relationship, and in particular the individual is no longer strictly defined through them relative to his family.[2] Their mobility and multi-functionality allow him to organize them more freely, and this reflects a greater openness in his social relationships. This, however, is only a partial liberation. So far as the serial object is concerned, in the absence of any restructuring of space, this 'functional' development is merely an emancipation, not (to go back to the old Marxian distinction) a liberation proper, for it implies *liberation from the function of the object only, not from the object itself.* Consider a nondescript, light, foldable table or a bed without legs, frame or canopy – an absolute cipher of a bed, one might say: all such objects, with their 'pure' outlines, no longer resemble even what they are; they have been stripped down to their most primitive essence as mere apparatus and, as it were, definitively secularized. What has been liberated in them – and what, in being liberated, has liberated something in man (or rather, perhaps, what man, in liberating himself, has liberated in them) – is their function. The function is no longer obscured by the moral theatricality of the old furniture; it is emancipated now from ritual, from ceremonial, from the entire ideology which used to make our surroundings into an opaque mirror of a reified human structure. Today, at last, these objects emerge absolutely clear about the purposes they serve. They are thus indeed free as *functional objects* – that is, they have the freedom to function, and (certainly so far as serial objects are concerned) that is practically the *only* freedom they have.[3]

2. We cannot help but wonder, however, whether he is not henceforward strictly defined through them relative to society at large. On this point, see 'Models and Series' below.
3. Similarly, the bourgeois and industrial revolution gradually freed the individual from his involvement with religion, morality and family. He thus acceded to a freedom in law as an individual, but also to an actual freedom as labour-power – that is, the freedom to sell himself as labour-power. This parallel has nothing coincidental about it, for there is a profound correlation here: both the serially produced 'functional' object and the social individual are liberated in their 'functional' objectification, not in their singularity or in their totality as object or person.

Now, *just so long as the object is liberated only in its function, man equally is liberated only as user of that object.* This too is progress, though not a decisive turning-point. A bed is a bed, a chair is a chair, and there is no relationship between them so long as each serves only the function it is supposed to serve. And without such a relationship there can be no space, for space exists only when it is opened up, animated, invested with rhythm and expanded by a correlation between objects and a transcendence of their functions in this new structure. In a way space is the object's true freedom, whereas its function is merely its formal freedom. The bourgeois dining-room was structured, but its structure was closed. The functional environment is more open, freer, but it is destructured, fragmented into its various functions. Somewhere between the two, in the gap between integrated psychological space and fragmented functional space, serial objects have their being, witnesses to both the one and the other – sometimes within a single interior.

The Model Interior

Modular Components
This elusive space, which is no longer either a confined externality nor an interior refuge, this freedom, this 'style' which is indecipherable in the serial object because it is subordinated to that object's function, may nevertheless be encountered in *model interiors,* which embody a new emerging structure and a significant evolution.[4]

Leafing through such glossy magazines as *Maison Française* or *Mobilier et Décoration* [Furniture and Decoration],[5] one cannot fail to notice two alternating themes. The first reaches for the

4. In other words, these things happen at a privileged level. And there is a sociological and a social problem with the fact that a restricted group should have the concrete freedom to present itself, through its objects and furniture, as a model in the eyes of an entire society. This problem will be addressed later, however – see 'Models and Series' below.
5. A glossy magazine devoted to mass-produced products is unthinkable, the only appropriate form here being a catalogue.

sublime, presenting houses beyond compare: old eighteenth-century mansions, miraculously well-equipped villas, Italian gardens heated by infra-red rays and populated by Etruscan statuettes – in short, the world of the unique, leaving the reader no alternative (so far as sociological generalization is concerned, at any rate) but contemplation without hope. Aristocratic models such as these, by virtue of their absolute value, are what underpin the second theme, that of modern interior decoration and furnishing. The objects and furniture proposed here, though they are high in 'status' value, do impinge on sociological reality: they are not dream creations without commercial significance but, rather, *models* in the proper sense of the word. We are no longer in a world of pure art, but in a world which (potentially, at least) is of interest to the whole of society.

These models of the home-furnishing avant-garde are organized around the basic distinction between COMPONENTS and SEATING; the practical imperative they obey is that of INTERIOR DESIGN, or syntagmatic calculation, to which may be contrasted, as seats are to components, the general concept of ATMOSPHERE.

TECMA: Extensible and interlocking components. Can be transformed or enlarged. Harmonious – they create a perfectly matching set of furniture. Functional – they answer all the needs of modern living. And they meet all your furnishing requirements – bookshelves, bar, radio, cupboards, wardrobe, desk space, cabinets, dresser, drawers, display unit, file storage, hideaway table . . .

TECMA is available in oiled teak or finished mahogany.

OSCAR: Put your OSCAR environment together with your own hands! Exciting! Unprecedented!

The OSCAR furniturama is a set of specially pre-cut components. Discover the fun of designing a miniature three-dimensional model of your furniture, in colour and just the right size to handle! You can build your model and change it around to your heart's content – all in the comfort of your own home!

Then, with perfect confidence, order your original and personal OSCAR furniture – soon to be the pride of your household!

MONOPOLY: Every MONOPOLY ensemble is your personality's best friend. A high-quality cabinetwork system, in teak or makoré. Jointing and assembling leave no traces. Four-sided components can be put together in an infinite variety of ways – an infinite variety of genuine furniture adapted to your own particular tastes, size requirements and needs.

These are multi-combinable single-block components. You're sure to want them so that you too can give your home that refined atmosphere you've been dreaming about.

These examples reveal how the functional object is being transcended by a new kind of practical organization. Symbolic values, and along with them use values, are being supplanted by organizational values. The substance and form of the old furniture have been abandoned for good, in favour of an extremely free interplay of functions. These objects are no longer endowed with a 'soul', nor do they invade us with their symbolic presence: the relationship has become an objective one, founded on disposition and play. The value this relationship takes on is no longer of an instinctive or a psychological but, rather, of a tactical kind. What such objects embody is no longer the secret of a unique relationship but, rather, differences, and moves in a game. The former radical closure has disappeared, in parallel with a distinct change in social and interpersonal structures.

Walls and Daylight
The rooms and the house themselves now transcend the traditional dividing-line of the wall, which formerly made them into spaces of refuge. Rooms open into one another, everything communicates, and space is broken up into angles, diffuse areas and mobile sectors. Rooms, in short, have been liberalized. Windows are no longer

imposed upon the free influx of air and light – a light which used to come *from outside* and settle upon objects, illuminating them *as though from within*. Now there are quite simply no windows, and a freely intervening light has become a universal function of the existence of things. In the same way objects have lost the substantiality which was their basis, the form which enclosed them whereby man made them part of his self-image: it is now space which plays freely between them, and becomes the universal function of their relationships and their 'values'.

Lighting

Many significant features of this general evolution might be pointed out. The tendency for light sources to be made invisible is a case in point. 'A recessed ceiling conceals perimeter neon fixtures for general diffuse lighting.' 'Uniform lighting is ensured by neon tubes concealed in various places: the full length of the recessed ceiling above the curtains, behind and all along the top rim of the built-in units, beneath the upper row of cupboards, etc.' Everything suggests that the source of light continues to be evocative of the origin of all things: even though it no longer illuminates the family circle from the ceiling, even though it has been dispersed and made manifold, it is apparently still the sign of a privileged intimacy, still able to invest things with unique value, to create shadows and invent presences. Small wonder that a system founded on the objective manipulation of simple and homogeneous elements should strive to eliminate this last sign of internal radiance, of the symbolic envelopment of things by look or desire.

Mirrors and Portraits

Another symptomatic change is the disappearance of looking-glasses and mirrors. A psycho-sociology of the mirror is overdue, especially in the wake of so much metaphysics. The traditional peasant milieu had no mirrors, perhaps even feared them as somewhat eerie. The bourgeois interior, by contrast, and what remains of that interior in present-day serially produced furniture, has mirrors in profusion, hung on the walls and incorporated into wardrobes, sideboards, cabinets or panelling. As a source of light, the mirror enjoys a special place in the room. This is the basis of the ideological role it has played, everywhere in the domestic world of the well-to-do, as redundancy, superfluity, reflection: the mirror is an opulent object which affords the self-indulgent bourgeois individual the opportunity to exercise his privilege – to reproduce his own image and revel in his possessions. In a more general sense we may say that the mirror is a symbolic object which not only reflects the characteristics of the individual but also echoes in its expansion the historical expansion of individual consciousness. It thus carries the stamp of approval of an entire social order: it is no coincidence that the century of Louis XIV is epitomized by the Hall of Mirrors at Versailles, nor that, in more recent times, the spread of mirrors in apartments coincided with the spread of the triumphal Pharisaism of bourgeois consciousness, from Napoleon III to Art Nouveau. But things have changed. There is no place in the functional ensemble for reflection for its own sake. The mirror still exists, but its most appropriate place is in the bathroom, unframed. There, dedicated to the fastidious care of the appearance that social intercourse demands, it is liberated from the graces and glories of domestic subjectivity. By the same token other objects are in turn liberated from mirrors; hence, they are no longer tempted to exist in a closed circuit with their own images. For mirrors close off space, presuppose a wall, refer back to the centre of the room. The more mirrors there are, the more glorious is the intimacy of the room, albeit more turned in upon itself. The current proliferation of openings and transparent partitions clearly represents a diametrically opposed approach. (Furthermore, all the tricks that mirrors make possible run counter to the current demand for a frank use of materials.) A chain has definitely been broken, and there is a real logic to the modern approach when it eliminates not only central or over-visible light sources but also the mirrors that used to reflect them; by thus eschewing any focus on or return to a central point, it frees space of the converging squint which gave bourgeois décor – much like bourgeois consciousness in general – such a cross-eyed view of itself.[6]

Something else, too, has disappeared in tandem with mirrors: the family portrait, the wedding photograph in the bedroom, the full-length or half-length portrait of the master of the house in the drawing-room, the framed close-ups of the children almost everywhere. All these, constituting a sort of diachronic mirror of the family, disappear along with mirrors themselves when a certain level of modernity is reached (although this has not happened as yet on any wide scale). Even works of art, whether originals or reproductions, no longer have a part to play as an absolute value, but merely in a combining mode. The success of prints as decoration in contrast to framed pictures is in part to be explained by their lower absolute value, and hence greater value in association. No object, any more than lights and mirrors, must be allowed to regain too intense a focus.

Clocks and Time

Another illusion forsworn by the modern interior is the illusion of time. An essential object has vanished: the clock. It is worth recalling that although the centre of the peasant room is the fire and fireplace, the clock is nevertheless a majestic and living element therein. In the bourgeois or petty-bourgeois interior it takes the form of the clock that so often crowns the marble mantelpiece, itself usually dominated by a mirror above – the whole ensemble constituting the most extraordinary symbolic résumé of bourgeois domesticity. The clock is to time as the mirror is to space. Just as the relationship to the reflected image institutes a closure and a kind of introjection of space, so the clock stands paradoxically for the permanence and introjection of time. Country clocks are among the most sought-after of objects,

6. The mirror occasionally makes a comeback, but it does so in a baroque cultural mode, as a secondary object – a romantic looking-glass, say, or an antique or bull's-eye mirror. The function is no longer the same (and will be addressed below apropos of antiques in general).

precisely because they capture time and strip it of surprises within the intimacy of a piece of furniture. There is nothing in the world more reassuring. The measuring of time produces anxiety when it serves to assign us to social tasks, but it makes us feel safe when it substantializes time and cuts it into slices like an object of consumption. Everybody knows from experience how intimate a ticking clock can make a place feel; the reason is that the clock's sound assimilates the place to the inside of our own body. The clock is a mechanical heart that reassures us about our own heart. It is precisely this process of infusion or assimilation of the substance of time, this presence of duration, which is rejected, just like all other returns to inwardness, by a modern order based on externality, spatiality and objective relationships.

Towards a Sociology of Interior Design?

It is the whole world of *Stimmung* that has disappeared, the world of 'natural' harmony between movements of the emotions and the presence of things: an internalized atmosphere as opposed to the externalized atmosphere of modern 'interiors'. Today, value resides neither in appropriation nor in intimacy but in information, in inventiveness, in control, in a continual openness to objective messages – in short, in the syntagmatic calculation which is, strictly speaking, the foundation of the discourse of the modern home-dweller.

The entire conception of decoration has changed too. Traditional good taste, which decided what was beautiful on the basis of secret affinities, no longer has any part here. That taste constituted a poetic discourse, an evocation of self-contained objects that responded to one another; today objects do not respond to one another, they communicate – they have no individual presence but merely, at best, an overall coherence attained by virtue of their simplification as components of a code and the way their relationships are calculated. An unrestricted combinatorial system enables man to use them as the elements of his structural discourse.

The System of Objects

Advertising widely promotes this new conception of decoration: 'Create a livable and well-organized three-room flat in 30 square metres!'; 'Multiply your flat by four!' More generally, it always talks of interior decorating in terms of problems and solutions, and it is here, rather than in 'good taste', that the current direction of decoration is to be found: it is no longer a matter of setting up a theatre of objects or creating an ambience, but of solving a problem, devising the subtlest possible response to a complicated set of conditions, mobilizing a space.

In the case of serial objects, the possibilities of this functional discourse are reduced. Objects and furniture of this kind are dispersed elements whose syntactic links are not evident; to the degree that they are arranged in a calculated way, the organizing principle is penury, and the objects appear impoverished in their abstraction. This is a necessary abstraction, however, for it provides the basis, at the level of the model, for the homogeneity of the elements in functional interaction. First of all man must stop mixing himself up with things and investing them with his own image; he will then be able, beyond the utility they have for him, to project onto them his game plan, his calculations, his discourse, and invest these manoeuvres themselves with the sense of a message to others, and a message to oneself. By the time this point is reached the mode of existence of 'ambient' objects will have changed completely, and *a sociology of furnishing will perforce have given way to a sociology of interior design.*[7]

7. Roland Barthes describes this new stage as it affects cars:

> . . . the uniformity of models seems to belie the very idea of technical performance, so 'normal' driving becomes the only possible field in which phantasies of power and invention can be invested. The car thus transfers its phantasied power to a specific set of practices. Since we can no longer tinker with the object itself, we are reduced to tinkering with the way it is driven . . . it is no longer the car's forms and functions that call forth human dreams but, rather, its handling, and before long, perhaps, we shall be writing not a mythology of the automobile but a mythology of driving. ('La voiture, projection de l'ego', *Réalités*, no. 213, October 1963)

Both the images and the discourse of advertising attest to this development: the discourse, by placing the subject directly on the stage as actor and manager, in both the indicative and the imperative moods; the images, to the contrary, by leaving the subject out, for his presence would, in a way, be an anachronism. The subject is himself the order he puts into things, and this order excludes redundancy: man has simply to remove himself from the picture. His presence has accomplished its task. What man now creates is a space, not a décor, and whereas the figure of the master of the house was a normal part – indeed, the clearest connotation – of the traditional décor, a signature is thoroughly alien to any 'functional' space.

Man the Interior Designer

We are beginning to see what the new model of the home-dweller looks like: 'man the interior designer' is neither an owner nor a mere user – rather, he is an active engineer of atmosphere. Space is at his disposal like a kind of distributed system, and by controlling this space he holds sway over all possible reciprocal relations between the objects therein, and hence over all the roles they are capable of assuming. (It follows that he must also be 'functional' himself: he and the space in question must be homogeneous if his messages of design are to leave him and return to him successfully.) What matters to him is neither possession nor enjoyment but responsibility, in the strict sense which implies that it is at all times possible for him to determine 'responses'. His praxis is exclusively external. This modern home-dweller does not 'consume' his objects. (Here again, 'taste' no longer has the slightest part to play, for in both its meanings it refers us back to self-contained objects whose form contains an 'edible' substance, so to speak, which makes them susceptible of internalization.) Instead of consuming objects, he dominates, controls and orders them. He discovers himself in the manipulation and tactical equilibration of a system.

There is clearly something abstract about this model of the 'functional' home-dweller. Advertising would like us to believe that modern man no longer fundamentally *needs* his objects, that all he has to do now is operate among them as an intelligent technician of communications. Our environment, however, is a *directly experienced* mode of existence, and it is very abstract indeed to apply to it computational and informational models borrowed from the purely technical realm. Furthermore, this objectivizing approach is accompanied by a cascade of ambiguous phraseology – 'to your own taste', 'to your own measurements', 'personalization', 'the atmosphere will be yours alone', and so forth – which appears to contradict that approach but in fact covers for it. The objective game which man the interior designer is invited to play is invariably taken over by the double-dealing of advertising. Yet the game's very logic conveys with it the image of a general strategy of human relations, the image of a human project, of a *modus vivendi* for the technical age – a genuine change of civilization whose impact may be discerned even in everyday life.

Consider the object for a moment: the object as humble and receptive supporting actor, as a sort of psychological slave or confidant – the object as directly experienced in traditional daily life and illustrated throughout the history of Western art down to our own day. This object was the reflection of a total order, bound up with a well-defined conception of décor and perspective, substance and form. According to this conception, the form is an absolute dividing-line between inside and outside. Form is a rigid container, and within it is substance. Beyond their practical function, therefore, objects – and specifically objects of furniture – have a primordial function as vessels, a function that belongs to the register of the imaginary.[8] This explains their psychological receptiveness. They are the reflection of a whole view of the

8. A law of dimension also seems to come into play, however, at the level of symbolic organization: any object above a certain size, even one with phallic significance (car, rocket), becomes a receptacle, vessel or womb, while any below a particular size becomes penile, even if it is a bowl or a knick-knack.

world according to which each being is a 'vessel of inwardness' and relations between beings are transcendent correlations of substances; thus the house itself is the symbolic equivalent of the human body, whose potent organic schema is later generalized into an ideal design for the integration of social structures. All this makes up a complete mode of life whose basic ordering principle is Nature as the original substance from which value is derived. In creating or manufacturing objects, man makes himself, through the imposition of a form (i.e. through culture), into the transubstantiator of nature. It is the passing down of substances from age to age, from form to form, which supplies the archetype of creativity, namely creation *ab utero* and the whole poetic and metaphorical symbolic system that goes with it.[9] So, with meaning and value deriving from the hereditary transmission of substances under the jurisdiction of form, the world is experienced as given (as it always is in the unconscious and in childhood), and the task is to reveal and perpetuate it. So too, with the form perfectly circumscribing the object, a portion of nature is included therein, just as in the case of the human body: the object on this view is essentially anthropomorphic. Man is thus bound to the objects around him by the same visceral intimacy, *mutatis mutandis*, that binds him to the organs of his own body, and 'ownership' of the object always tends virtually towards the appropriation of its substance by oral annexation and 'assimilation'.

What we glimpse today in modern interiors is the coming end of this order of Nature; what is appearing on the horizon, beyond the break-up of form, beyond the dissolution of the formal boundary between inside and outside and of the whole dialectic of being and appearance relating to that boundary, is a qualitatively new kind of relationship, a new kind of objective responsibility. As directly experienced, the project of a technological

9. Intellectual and artistic production, traditionally seen in terms of gifts, inspiration or genius, has never really been anything more than an echo of this archetype.

society implies putting the very idea of genesis into question and omitting all the origins, received meanings and 'essences' of which our old pieces of furniture remained concrete symbols; it implies practical computation and conceptualization on the basis of a total abstraction, the notion of a world no longer given but instead produced – mastered, manipulated, inventoried, controlled: a world, in short, that has to be *constructed*.[10]

Although it is different in kind from the traditional procreative order, this modern order nevertheless also depends on a basic symbolic system. Whereas the earlier civilization, founded on the natural order of substances, may be said to have been underpinned by oral structures, the modern order of production, calculation and functionality must be viewed as a phallic order linked to the enterprise whose goal is the supersession and transformation of the given and the opening up of new objective structures; but it is at the same time a faecal order founded on an abstraction or quintessence meant to inform a homogeneous material world, on the measuring off and division of material reality, on a great anal aggressiveness sublimated into play, discourse, ordering, classifying and placement.

The organizing of things, even when in the context of technical enterprise it has every appearance of being objective, always remains a powerful springboard for projection and cathexis. The best evidence of this is the obsessiveness that lies behind so many organizational projects and (of most relevance to our present discussion) behind the will to design. Everything has to intercommunicate, everything has to be functional – no more secrets, no more mysteries, everything is organized, therefore everything is clear. This is not the old slogan of the house-proud:

10. As a matter of fact this model of praxis emerges clearly only when a high technical level has been attained, or in the context of very advanced everyday objects, such as tape recorders, cars or household appliances, whose dials, dashboards or control panels bespeak the degree of mastery and coordination required to operate them. It should be noted that everyday life is still very largely governed by the traditional forms of praxis.

a place for everything and everything in its place. That obsession was moral, today's is functional – and explicable in terms of the faecal function, which requires absolute conductivity in all internal organs. Here we have the basis for a character profile of technical civilization: if hypochondria is an obsession with the circulation of substances and the functioning of the primary organs, we might well describe modern man, the cybernetician, as a mental hypochondriac, as someone obsessed with the perfect circulation of messages.

II Structures of Atmosphere

The term 'interior design' sums up the organizational aspect of the domestic environment, but it does not cover the entire system of the modern living space, which is based on a counterpoint between DESIGN and ATMOSPHERE. In the discourse of advertising the technical need for design is always accompanied by the cultural need for atmosphere. The two structure a single practice; they are two aspects of a single *functional* system. And both mobilize the values of play and of calculation – calculation of function in the case of design, calculation of materials, forms and space in the case of atmosphere.[11]

Atmospheric Values: Colour

Traditional Colour

In the traditional system colours have psychological and moral overtones. A person will 'like' a particular colour, or have 'their' colour. Colour may be dictated by an event, a ceremony, or a social role; alternatively, it may be the characteristic of a particular material – wood, leather, canvas or paper. Above all it remains circumscribed by form; it does not seek contact with other colours, and it is not a free value. Tradition confines colours to its own parochial meanings and draws the strictest of boundary-lines about them. Even in the freer ceremonial of fashion, colours generally

---

11. To the extent that arrangement involves dealing with space, it too may be considered a component of atmosphere.

derive their significance from outside themselves: they are simply metaphors for fixed cultural meanings. At the most impoverished level, the symbolism of colours gets lost in mere psychological resonance: red is passionate and aggressive, blue a sign of calm, yellow optimistic, and so on; and by this point the language of colours is little different from the languages of flowers, dreams or the signs of the Zodiac.

The traditional treatment of colour negates colour as such, rejects it as a complete value. Indeed, the bourgeois interior reduces it for the most part to discreet 'tints' and 'shades'. Grey, mauve, garnet, beige – all the shades assigned to velours, woollens and satins, to the profusion of fabrics, curtains, carpets and hangings, as also to heavier materials and 'period' forms, imply a moral refusal of both colour and space. But especially of colour, which is deemed too spectacular, and a threat to inwardness. The world of colours is opposed to the world of values, and the 'chic' invariably implies the elimination of appearances in favour of being:[12] black, white, grey – whatever registers zero on the colour scale – is correspondingly paradigmatic of dignity, repression, and moral standing.

'Natural' Colour

Colours would not celebrate their release from this anathema until very late. It would be generations before cars and typewriters came in anything but black, and even longer before refrigerators and washbasins broke with their universal whiteness. It was painting that liberated colour, but it still took a very long time for the effects to register in everyday life. The advent of bright red armchairs, sky-blue settees, black tables, multicoloured kitchens, living-rooms in two or three different tones, contrasting inside walls, blue or pink façades (not to mention mauve and black underwear)

12. 'Loud' colours are meant to strike the eye. If you wear a red suit, you are more than naked – you become a pure object with no inward reality. The fact that women's tailored suits tend to be in bright colours is a reflection of the social status of women as objects.

suggests a liberation stemming from the overthrow of a global order. This liberation, moreover, was contemporary with that of the functional object (with the introduction of synthetic materials, which were polymorphous, and of non-traditional objects, which were polyfunctional). The transition, however, did not go smoothly. Colour that loudly announced itself as such soon began to be perceived as over-aggressive, and before long it was excluded from model forms, whether in clothing or in furnishing, in favour of a somewhat relieved return to discreet tones. There is a kind of obscenity of colour which modernity, after exalting it briefly as it did the explosion of form, seems to end up apprehending in much the same way as it apprehends pure functionality: labour should not be discernible anywhere – neither should instinct be allowed to show its face. The dropping of sharp contrasts and the return to 'natural' colours as opposed to the violence of 'affected' colours reflects this compromise solution at the level of model objects. At the level of serially produced objects, by contrast, bright colour is always apprehended as a sign of emancipation – in fact it often compensates for the absence of more fundamental qualities (particularly a lack of space). The discrimination here is obvious: associated with primary values, with functional objects and synthetic materials, bright, 'vulgar' colours always tend to predominate in the serial interior. They thus partake of the same anonymity as the functional object: having once represented something approaching a liberation, both have now become signs that are merely traps, raising the banner of freedom but delivering none to direct experience.

Furthermore – and this is their paradox – such straightforward and 'natural' colours turn out to be neither. They turn out to be nothing but an impossible echo of the state of nature, which explains why they are so aggressive, why they are so naïve – and why they so very quickly take refuge in an order which, for all that it is no longer the old moral order with its complete rejection of colour, is nevertheless a puritanical order of compromise with nature. This is the order, or reign, of *pastels*. Clothing, cars, showers, household appliances, plastic surfaces – nowhere here, it seems, is the 'honest' colour that painting once liberated as a living force now to be found. Instead we encounter only the pastels, which aspire to be living colours but are in fact merely *signs* for them, complete with a dash of moralism.

All the same, even though these two compromises, the flight into black and white and the flight into pastels, ultimately voice the same disavowal of pure colour as the direct expression of instinctual life, they do not do so in accordance with the same system. The first is systematized by reference to an unequivocally moral and anti-natural black/white paradigm, whereas the pastel solution answers to a system with a larger register founded *not on opposition to nature but on naturalness.* Nor do the two systems have the same function. Black (or grey) retains the meaning of distinction, of culture, as opposed to the whole range of vulgar colours.[13] As for white, it remains largely pre-eminent in the 'organic' realm: bathrooms, kitchens, sheets, linen – anything that is bound up with the body and its immediate extensions has for generations been the domain of white, a surgical, virginal colour which distances the body from the dangers of intimacy and tends to neutralize the drives. It is also in this unavoidable area of hygiene and down-to-earth tasks that the use of synthetic materials, such as light metals, formica, nylon, plastiflex, aluminium, and so forth, has experienced its most rapid growth and achieved a dominant position. Of course the lightness and practical utility of these materials have much to do with their success, but the very convenience they offer does not merely lighten the burden of work, it also helps to drain value from this whole basic area. The fluid, simplified lines of our refrigerators or similar machines, with their plastic or artificial lightweight material, operate likewise as a kind of 'whiteness' – as a non-stressed indicator of the presence of

13. Already, however, there are quite a few cars that are simply no longer available in black; apart from mourning or other ceremonial uses, black has almost completely disappeared from American life (except where it is brought back as a combining element).

these objects that bespeaks the radical omission from our consciousness of the responsibilities they imply, and of bodily functions in general, which are never innocent. Little by little colour is making inroads here, too, but resistance to this development is very deeply felt. In any case, even if kitchens are blue or yellow, even if bathrooms are pink (or even black – a 'snobbish' black as a reaction to the former 'moral' white), we may still justifiably ask to what nature such colours allude. For even if they do not turn pastel, they do connote a kind of nature, one that has its own history: the 'nature' of leisure time and holidays.

It is not 'real' nature which suddenly transfigures the atmosphere of daily life, but holidays – that simulacrum of nature, the reverse side of everyday routine, thriving not on nature but on the Idea of Nature. It is holidays that serve as a model here, holidays whose colours devolve into the primary everyday realm. And it was indeed in the fake natural environment of holidays, with its caravan, tents and camping gear, experienced as a model and as a zone of freedom, that the tendency towards bright colours, to plasticity, to the ephemeral practicality of labour-saving gadgets, and so on, first came to the fore. We began by transplanting our little house into Nature, only to end up bringing the values of leisure and the idea of Nature back home with us. There has been a sort of flight of objects into the sphere of leisure: freedom and the absence of responsibilities are thus inscribed both in colours and in the transitory and insignificant character of materials and forms.

'Functional' Colour

Thus, after a few brief episodes of violent liberation (notably in the world of art, with, in the end, but mild impact upon everyday life – except, of course, for the spheres of advertising and commerce, where colour's power to corrupt enjoys full rein), colour was immediately taken back in hand by a system in *which nature no longer plays any part except as naturalness* – as a mere connotation of nature behind whose screen instinctual values continue to be subtly disavowed. Nevertheless, the very abstractness of these now 'free' colours means that they are at last able to play an active role. It is towards this third stage that colour is at present orientating itself so far as model objects are concerned: a stage characterized by colour as an atmospheric value. Certainly an 'atmospheric' interplay of this kind is already prefigured in the colours associated with leisure, but these colours still refer too clearly to a system directly experienced, namely holidays and the primary level of everyday life; consequently they are subject to external constraints. In the fully fledged system of atmosphere, by contrast, colours obey no principle but that of their own interaction; no longer constrained in any way, whether by ethical considerations or by nature, they answer to one imperative only – the gauging of atmosphere.

Indeed, in a sense we are no longer dealing with colours *per se* but with more abstract values. The combination, matching and contrast of tones are the real issues when it comes to the relationship between colour and atmosphere. Blue can go with green – all colours are capable of combination – but only certain blues with certain greens; furthermore, it is not so much a question of blue and green as one of *hot and cold*. At the same time, colour is no longer a way of emphasizing each object by setting it off from the décor; colours are now contrasting ranges of shades, their value has less and less to do with their sensory qualities, they are often dissociated from their form, and it is their tonal differences that give a room its 'rhythm'. Just as modular furniture loses its specific functions so much that at the logical extreme its value resides solely in the positioning of each movable element, so likewise colours lose their unique value, and become relative to each other and to the whole. This is what is meant by describing them as 'functional'.

Consider the following descriptions from a practical guide to interior decoration:

The framework of the seats has been painted in the same shade as the walls, while the shade chosen for the upholstery echoes that of the hangings. There is harmony between the cold tones, off-white and blue, but certain touches supply the necessary warm response: the gold frame of the Louis XVI mirror, the light-coloured wood of the table, the parquet floor, and the bright red of the carpets. Red here constitutes a sort of upward movement – the red of the carpet, the red of the seats, the red of the cushions – to which is opposed a downward movement in the blues of hangings, settees and chairs.[14]

A plain matte white background interrupted by great blue surfaces (on the ceiling). White and blue are repeated in the arrangement of the décor: a white marble table, a screen partition. . . . A warm touch is supplied by the bright red doors of a low storage unit. In fact we find ourselves in a space handled entirely in plain colours, devoid of any nuances of tone or of any softness (all the softness having taken refuge in the picture on the left), albeit balanced by large areas of white.[15]

Here is another example: 'The little indoor tropical garden is not just protected but also lent rhythm by a slab of black enamelled glass.' (Notice that black and white in these descriptions retain nothing of their traditional value; they have escaped from the white-black polarity and taken on a *tactical* value within the extended range of all colours.) When one considers the advice to 'choose a particular colour because your wall is large or small, because it contains such and such a number of doors, because your furniture is antique or modern, or designed in a European or an exotic tradition, or for some other precise reason',[16] it becomes clear that the third stage we have been discussing is indeed characterized by an objectivity of colour; strictly speaking, colour is now one more or less complex factor among others – just one element of a solution. Once again, this is what makes colour

14. Betty Pepys, *Le guide pratique de la décoration*, p. 163.
15. Ibid., p. 179.
16. Ibid., p. 191.

'functional' – that is to say, reduced to an abstract conceptual instrument of calculation.

Hot and Cold

So far as colours are concerned, 'atmosphere' depends upon a calculated balance between hot and cold tones. This is a fundamental distinction which – along with a few others (components/seats,[17] design/atmosphere) – helps to endow the discursive system of furnishing with a high degree of coherence, and thus makes it into a determining category of the overall system of objects. (We shall see that this coherence is perhaps merely that of a manifest discourse beneath which a latent discourse is continually deploying its contradictions.) To get back to the warmth of warm tones: this is clearly not a warmth grounded in confidence, intimacy or affection, nor an organic warmth emanating from colours or substances. Warmth of that kind once had its own density and required no opposing cold tones to define it negatively. Nowadays, on the other hand, both warm and cold tones are required to interact, in each ensemble, with structure and form. When we read that 'The warmth of its materials lends intimacy to this well-designed bureau', or when we are told of 'doors of matte oiled Brazilian rosewood traversed by chrome-plated handles [and] chairs covered in a buff leatherette that blends them perfectly into this austere and warm ensemble', we find that warmth is always contrasted with rigour, organization, structure, or something of the sort, and that every 'value' is defined by this contrast between two poles. 'Functional' warmth is thus a warmth that no longer issues forth from a warm substance, nor from a harmonious juxtaposition of particular objects, but instead arises from the systematic oscillation or abstract synchrony of a perpetual 'warm-and-cold' which in reality continually defers any real 'warm' feeling. This is a purely *signified* warmth – hence one which, by definition, is never realized: a warmth characterized, precisely, by the absence of any source.

17. See below, pp. 44 ff.

Atmospheric Values: Materials

Natural Wood/Cultural Wood

The same sort of analysis applies to materials – to wood, for example, so sought after today for nostalgic reasons. Wood draws its substance from the earth, it lives and breathes and 'labours'. It has its latent warmth; it does not merely reflect, like glass, but burns from within. Time is embedded in its very fibres, which makes it the perfect container, because every content is something we want to rescue from time. Wood has its own odour, it ages, it even has parasites, and so on. In short, it is a material that has *being*. Think of the notion of 'solid oak' – a living idea for each of us, evoking as it does the succession of generations, massive furniture and ancestral family homes. The question we must ask, however, is whether this 'warmth' of wood (or likewise the 'warmth' of freestone, natural leather, unbleached linen, beaten copper, or any of the elements of the material and maternal dream that now feeds a high-priced nostalgia) still has any meaning.

By now functional substitutes for virtually all organic and natural materials have been found in the shape of plastic and polymorphous substances: wool, cotton, silk and linen are thus all susceptible of replacement by nylon and its countless variants, while wood, stone and metal are giving way to concrete and polystyrene.[18] There can be no question of rejecting this tendency and simply dreaming of the ideal warm and human substance of the objects of former times. The distinction between natural and

18. This development at least partially realizes the substantialist myth which, beginning in the sixteenth century, informed the stucco and the worldly demiurgy of the baroque style: the notion that the whole world could be cast from a single ready-made material. This substantialist myth is one aspect of the functionalist myth that I discuss elsewhere, and the equivalent on the material plane of automatism on the functional one. The idea is that a 'machine of machines' would replace all human gestures and institute a synthetic universe. It should be borne in mind, however, that the 'substantialist' dream is the most primitive and repressive aspect of the myth as a whole, for it continues to enshrine a pre-mechanist alchemy of transubstantiation.

synthetic substances, just like that between traditional colours and bright colours, is strictly a value judgement. Objectively, substances are simply what they are: there is no such thing as a true or a false, a natural or an artificial substance. How could concrete be somehow less 'authentic' than stone? We apprehend *old* synthetic materials such as paper as altogether natural – indeed, glass is one of the richest substances we can conceive of. In the end, the inherited nobility of a given material can exist only for a cultural ideology analogous to that of the aristocratic myth itself in the social world – and even that cultural prejudice is vulnerable to the passage of time.

The point is to understand, apart from the vast horizons opened up on the practical level by these new substances, just how they have changed the 'meaning' of the materials we use.

Just as the shift to shades (warm, cold or intermediate) means that colours are stripped of their moral and symbolic status in favour of an abstract quality which makes their systematization and interplay possible, so likewise the manufacture of synthetics means that materials lose their symbolic naturalness and become polymorphous, so achieving a higher degree of abstractness which makes possible a universal play of associations among materials, and hence too a transcendence of the formal antithesis between natural and artificial materials. There is thus no longer any difference 'in nature' between a Thermoglass partition and a wooden one, between rough concrete and leather: whether they embody 'warm' or 'cold' values, they all now have exactly the same status as component materials. These materials, though disparate in themselves, are nevertheless homogeneous as cultural signs, and thus susceptible of organization into a coherent system. Their abstractness makes it possible to combine them at will.[19]

19. And this is the difference, for instance, between the 'solid oak' of old and the present-day use of teak. Teak is not fundamentally distinct from oak in respect of origin, exoticism or cost; it is its use in the creation of atmosphere which means that it is no longer a primary natural material, dense and warm, but, rather, *a mere cultural sign of such warmth*, and by virtue of that fact reinstated *qua* sign, like so many other 'noble' materials, in the system of the modern interior: no longer wood-as-material but wood-as-component. And now, instead of the quality of presence, it has atmospheric value.

The Logic of Atmosphere

This 'discourse of atmosphere' concerning colours, substance, volume, space, and so on mobilizes all these elements simultaneously in a great systematic reorganization: it is because furniture now comprises movable elements in a decentralized space, and because it has a correspondingly lighter structure based on assembly and veneers, that there is a case for more 'abstract' woods – teak, mahogany, rosewood or certain Scandinavian woods.[20] And it so happens that the colours of these woods are not traditional either, but lighter or darker variations, often varnished, lacquered, or left deliberately unfinished; the main point, though, is that the colour in question, like the wood itself, is always *abstract* – an object of mental manipulation along with everything else. The entire modern environment is thus transposed onto the level of a sign system, namely ATMOSPHERE, which is no longer produced by the way any particular element is handled, nor by the beauty or ugliness of that element. That used to be true for the inconsistent and subjective system of tastes and colours, of *de gustibus non est disputandum*, but under the present system the success of the whole occurs in the context of the constraints of abstraction and association.

Whether or not you care for teak, for example, you are obliged to acknowledge that its use is consistent with the organization of component elements, that its shade is consistent with a plane surface, hence also with a particular 'rhythm' of space, etc., etc. – and that this is indeed the law of the system. There is nothing at all – not antiques, not rustic furniture in solid wood, not even precious or craft objects – that cannot be incorporated into the interactions of the system, thus attesting to the boundless possi-

20. Certainly these woods are technically better suited than oak to the needs of veneering and assembling. It must also be said that exoticism plays the same role here as the idea of holidays does in the use of bright colours: it evokes the myth of an escape via 'naturalness'. The essential point, however, is that for all these reasons these woods are 'secondary' woods, embodying a cultural abstraction that enables them to partake of the logic of the system.

bilities of such abstract integration. The current proliferation of such objects does not constitute a contradiction in the system:[21] they enter the system precisely as the most 'modern' materials and colours, and as atmospheric elements. Only a traditional and fundamentally naïve view would find inconsistency in the encounter, on a teak-veneered chest, of a futuristic cube in raw metal and the rotten wood of a sixteenth-century carving. The point is, though, that *the consistency here is not the natural consistency of a unified taste but the consistency of a cultural system of signs.* Not even a 'Provençal' room, not even an authentic Louis XVI drawing-room, can attest to anything beyond a vain nostalgic desire to escape from the modern cultural system: both are just as far removed from the 'style' they ape as any formica-topped table or any black-metal and leatherette tubular chair. An exposed ceiling beam is every bit as abstract as a chrome-plated tube or an Emauglas partition. What nostalgia paints as an authentic whole object is still nothing but a combining variant, as is indeed signalled by the language used in speaking of provincial or period 'ensembles'. The word 'ensemble', closely related to 'atmosphere', serves to reintroduce any conceivable element, whatever subjective associations it may carry, into the logic of the system. That this system is affected by ideological connotations and latent motives is indisputable, and we shall return to this question later. But it is incontestable, too, that its logic, which is that of a combination of signs, is irreversible and limitless. No object can escape this logic, just as no product can escape the formal logic of the commodity.

A Model Material: Glass

One material sums up the idea of atmosphere and may be thought of as embodying a universal function in the modern environment. That material is GLASS. Advertising calls it 'the material of the future' – a future which, as we all know, will itself be 'transparent'.

---

21. It does indicate a *shortcoming* of the system – but a successfully integrated one. On this point, see the discussion of antiques below.

The System of Objects

Glass is thus both the material used and the ideal to be achieved, both end and means. So much for metaphysics. Psychologically speaking, glass in its practical, as in its imaginary uses has many merits. It is the ideal modern recipient: it does not 'pick up the taste', it does not change over time as a function of its content, as do wood and metal, nor does it shroud that content in mystery. Glass eliminates all confusion in short order, and does not conduct heat. Fundamentally it is less a recipient than an isolator – the miracle of a rigid fluid – a content that is also a container, and hence the basis of a transparency between the two: a kind of transcendence which, as we have seen, is the first priority in the creation of atmosphere. Moreover, glass implies a symbolism of access to a secondary state of consciousness, and at the same time it is ranked symbolically at zero level on the scale of materials. Its symbolism is one of solidification – hence of abstractness. This abstractness opens the door to the abstractness of the inner world: the crystal of madness; to the abstractness of the future: the clairvoyant's crystal ball; and to the abstractness of nature: the other worlds to which the eye gains entry via microscope or telescope. And certainly, with its indestructibility, immunity to decay, colourlessness, odourlessness, and so on, glass exists at a sort of zero level of matter: glass is to matter as a vacuum is to air. We have already noted the operation of the values of play and calculation, combined with abstraction, apropos of the system of atmosphere. Above all, though, glass is the most effective conceivable material expression of the fundamental ambiguity of 'atmosphere': the fact that it is at once proximity and distance, intimacy and the refusal of intimacy, communication and non-communication. Whether as packaging, window or partition, glass is the basis of a transparency without transition: we see, but cannot touch. The message is universal and abstract. A shop window is at once magical and frustrating – the strategy of advertising in epitome. The transparency of jars containing food products implies a formal satisfaction, a kind of visual collusion, yet basically the relationship is one of exclusion. Glass works exactly like atmosphere in that it allows nothing but the *sign* of its content to emerge, in that it interposes itself in its transparency, just as the system of atmosphere does in its abstract consistency, between the materiality of things and the materiality of needs. Not to mention glass's cardinal virtue, which is of a moral order: its purity, reliability and objectivity, along with all those connotations of hygiene and prophylaxis which make it truly the material of the future – a future, after all, that is to be one of disavowal of the body, and of the primary and organic functions, in the name of a radiant and functional objectivity (of which hygiene is the moral version for the body).

> Live in a garden in close intimacy with nature – experience the charm of every season totally, without giving up the comforts of a modern living space. This is the new heaven on earth, the grace bestowed by houses with picture windows.

> Glass tile or block set in concrete makes it possible to construct translucent walls, partitions, arches and ceilings that are as strong as if they were built of stone. Such 'transpartitions' allow the passage of light, which is thus able freely to permeate the whole house. But, since the glass used is not see-through, the privacy of each room is preserved.

Clearly the age-old symbolism of the 'house of glass' is still with us, even though in the modern version it has lost much of its sublime aspect. *The distinction accorded transcendence has given way to that accorded atmosphere* (just as in the case of mirrors). Glass facilitates faster communication between inside and outside, yet at the same time it sets up an invisible but material caesura which prevents such communication from becoming a real opening onto the world. Indeed, the modern 'house of glass' does not open onto the outside at all; instead it is the outside world, nature, landscape, that penetrates, thanks to glass and its abstractness, into the intimate or private realm inside, and there 'plays freely' as a component of atmosphere. The whole world thus becomes integrated as spectacle into the domestic universe.[22]

The Man of Relationship and Atmosphere

From the foregoing account of colours and materials we may already draw a number of conclusions. The systematic alternation between hot and cold is fundamentally a defining trait of the concept of 'atmosphere' itself, for *atmosphere is always both warmth and distance.*

The 'atmospheric' interior is designed to permit the same alternation between warmth and non-warmth, between intimacy and distance, to operate not only between the objects that comprise it but also between the human beings who live in it. Friend or relative, family or customer – *some* relationship is always required, but it is supposed to remain mobile and

22. The ambiguity of glass becomes especially clear when we shift our focus from living-spaces to consumption and packaging – areas where its use is ever on the increase. Here too glass has all the desirable qualities: it protects the product against deterioration, letting nothing in but the appraising glance. 'To contain the product properly and let it be seen': a perfect definition of the goal of packaging. Mouldable to any form, glass offers unlimited options from the aesthetic point of view. We may confidently expect that before long it will be used to 'present' fruit and vegetables, ensuring that they remain as fresh as the morning dew. Very likely it will soon be enclosing even ordinary steaks with its transparent sheath. Invisible yet ubiquitous, it will constitute the ideal analogue of a more beautiful and limpidly clear life. Further, whatever purpose it may serve, glass can never become true refuse because it is without odour. It is a 'noble' material. All the same, the consumer is invited to throw it out after using it: 'No deposit – no return'. Glass thus cloaks the purchase in its 'indestructible' prestige – yet must be destroyed immediately. Is there a contradiction here? Not really, because glass is still playing its part as a component of atmosphere, but in this case 'atmosphere' has attained its full economic meaning, that of *packaging*. Glass sells things, it is functional in that sense, but it must also be consumed itself and, indeed, consumed at an accelerated rate. The psychological function of glass (its transparency and purity) is thus totally recuperated and submerged by its economic function. The sublime ends up as a motivation to buy.

'functional'; in other words, the aim is that relating should be possible at every instant, but its subjective aspects should no longer be problematic, and the various relationships should therefore be freely interchangeable. Such is the nature of functional relationships, from which desire is (in theory) absent, having been neutralized for the sake of atmosphere.[23] This, however, is where ambiguity begins.[24]

Seats

This ambiguity is attested to by the objects that best express the relationship of atmosphere: *seats*, which we see continually alternating in the system of modern furnishing with modular *components*. These antithetical kinds of objects concretize the opposition between the concepts of interior design and atmosphere (although they do not constitute the sole underpinnings of that opposition).

The minimal function of the countless seats that fill the furnishing and home-decorating magazines is unquestionably to permit people to sit down: to sit down to rest, or sit down at a table to eat. But chairs no longer gravitate towards a table; these days seats take on their own meaning, while tables – typically low coffee tables – are subordinate to them. This meaning, moreover, refers not to the posture of the body but to the position of interlocutors relative to each other. The general arrangement of the seating and slight changes in people's positions in the course of an evening may be said, for example, to constitute a discourse in themselves. Modern seating – pouf

23. Even sexuality itself in its modern conception is subsumed by the functional relationship. As distinct from sensuality, which is warm and instinctual, sexuality is at once HOT AND COLD – by virtue of this it ceases to be a passion and becomes nothing but an atmospheric value.
24. In the system of objects, as in all directly experienced systems, the major structural antitheses are always in effect more complicated than they seem, for what appears as a structural antithesis from the standpoint of the system may well be simply a consistent rationalization of an underlying conflict.

or settee, wall-sofa or easy chair – invariably lays the stress on sociability and conversation, promoting a sort of all-purpose position, appropriate to the modern social human being, which de-emphasizes everything in the sitting posture that suggests confrontation. No more beds for lying in, no more chairs for sitting at[25] – instead, 'functional' seats which treat all positions, and hence all human relationships, as a free synthesis. All moral overtones are gone: one no longer sits opposite anyone. It is impossible to become angry in such seats, or to argue, or to seek to persuade. They dictate a relaxed social interaction which makes no demands, which is open-ended but above all open to play. From their depths one is no longer obliged to meet another person's gaze or to look directly at them: these seats are so designed that one's eyes are entitled simply to look people over in a general way, for their positioning and depth combine to keep everyone's eye level 'naturally' at half the usual altitude – at an ill-defined elevation which is also that of the flow of words. Seats of this kind may well respond to a basic current concern, namely the wish never to be alone – but never to be face to face with another person either. The body is invited to relax, but it is above all the gaze, with all its perils, that must be put out to grass. Even as modern society frees us in large measure from the promiscuity of primary functions, it exacerbates the promiscuity of secondary ones, especially that of the gaze and its tragic dimension. Accordingly, just as primary demands are veiled, so likewise every effort is made to relieve social intercourse of all its rough edges, contradictoriness and, ultimately, obscenity – what is obscene here being the direct play of aggression and desire in the gaze.

The binary opposition between 'components' and 'seats' thus amounts to a complete system: modular components are the vehicle of modern man's organizing discourse, while from the

25. Except for chairs at the dining-table – which are upright and have peasant-like overtones. But this evidences a reflex cultural process.

depths of his chairs he proffers a discourse of relationship.[26] So 'man the interior designer' is always coupled with the 'man of relationship and atmosphere', and the two together give us 'functional man'.

Cultural Connotation and Censorship

For seats, then, but also for all other objects, cultural connotation is now as essential a requirement as calculation. In earlier times furniture stated its function. The fundamental nurturing function of the house found unequivocal expression in tables and side-boards that were heavy, round-bellied – overloaded with connota-tions of motherhood. Furniture whose function was taboo was flatly withdrawn from view, as in the case of a bed concealed in an alcove. As for the bed in the middle of the room, it was even more eloquent in its embodiment of bourgeois marriage (and not, of course, of sexuality). Today the bed is no more – in its place we

---

26. Or perhaps, after all, simply a *passive* discourse – for we should not forget that advertising is far less inclined to enjoin the active arrangement of furniture than to stress the passive joys of relaxation. On this point the notion of atmosphere is similarly ambiguous, for it has both active and passive implications. 'Functional man' is exhausted from the start. And the millions of leather and Dunlopillo armchairs, each deeper than the last, whose modern virtues of atmosphere and repose fill the pages of the glossy magazines, amount to a sort of massive invitation from our future civilization to resolve all our tensions and bask in a placid seventh-day euphoria. The whole ideology of that civilization – still far distant, yet imminent in model objects – is to be found in these images of an idyllic, neo-pastoral modernity in which the inhabitant communes with his atmosphere from the mellow depths of his chair. Having solved the problems of his emotions, his functions and his contradictions, so that all that is left are relationships, a system of relationships whose structure he rediscovers in a system of objects; having infused the space around him with life and 'created' a multiplicity of ways to integrate his modules into the room as a whole (much as he himself is integrated into the social whole); having thus put together a world absolved of drives and primary functions but overloaded with social connotations of calculation and prestige – having done all this, and tired out by his efforts, the modern home-dweller is ready to cosset his ennui by plunging into an easy chair whose form is a perfect match for the form of his body.

have only couches, divans, settees and banquettes. Some 'beds' now disappear into the wall, bowing not to moral stricture but to abstract logic.[27] Tables are low, no longer centrally placed, weightless. The whole kitchen has lost its culinary function and is now a functional laboratory. This is progress, moreover, because the traditional environment, for all its directness, was an environment of moral obsession that bespoke the material difficulty of living. We do have more freedom in the modern interior, but this freedom is accompanied by a subtler formalism and a new moralism: everything here indicates the obligatory shift from eating, sleeping and procreating to smoking, drinking, entertaining, discussing, looking and reading. Visceral functions have given way to functions determined by culture. The sideboard used to hold linen, crockery or food; the functional elements of today house books, knick-knacks, a cocktail bar, or nothing at all. The term 'refined' – which, like 'functional', is a catchword of manipulated interior decoration – sums up this cultural constraint perfectly. Rooms have traded in the symbols of family for signs of social relationship. Once a solemn backdrop for affection, they are now an equally ritualistic décor of reception. A close reading of modern house-furnishings reveals that they converse among themselves with an ease in every way comparable to that of the dinner guests, that they mingle and drift apart with the very same freedom, and that they convey the same message: namely, that it is quite possible to live without working.

Of course, culture has always played the ideological role of pacifier, sublimating tensions associated with functional imperatives and answering the need for being to take on recognizable form beyond the material reality and conflicts of the world. Such a form – which attests, despite everything, to the existence of a purpose, and ensures the direct memory of a fundamental security

27. An exception here is an object reintroduced with a new connotation that occludes its earlier obscenity, a case in point being the old free-standing eighteenth-century Spanish bed. (See the discussion of antiques below.)

– is no doubt even more urgently needed in a technological civilization. It is just that, like the reality it simultaneously reflects and disavows, this form is now being systematized. Systematic technicity calls forth systematic cultural connotation. And *this systematic cultural connotation at the level of objects is what I am calling ATMOSPHERE.*

Atmospheric Values: Gestural Systems and Forms

When we come, in our continuing analysis of atmospheric values, to the consideration of 'functional' forms (variously described as 'contoured', 'dynamic', etc.), we find that the 'stylization' of such forms cannot be disentangled from the stylization of the human gestural systems which correspond to them. The style of such gestural systems always implies the suppression of muscular energy, of labour. Primary functions are overwritten by secondary ones, by relationship and calculation, and instinctual drives give way to cultural connotation. All these tendencies are mediated practically and historically, at the level of objects, by the fundamental supersession of the gestural system of effort, by *the great shift from a universal gestural system of labour to a universal gestural system of control.* This is the turning-point at which a status enjoyed by objects for millennia, their anthropomorphic status, is definitively terminated – destroyed by the new abstractness of energy sources.

The Traditional Gestural System: Effort

So long as the energy applied was muscular in character, and hence immediate and contingent, the tool remained embedded in human relations, rich symbolically speaking but not particularly well designed structurally. The adoption of animals as a source of power did not represent a qualitative change: for entire civilizations human and animal power were essentially on a par. The unchanging nature of the energy employed meant that tools, too, underwent little change. Thus the status of the tool or manual object varied hardly at all over the centuries. Man's profound gestural relationship to objects, which epitomizes his integration into the world, into social structures, can be a highly fulfilling one, and this fulfilment is discernible in the beauty – the 'style' – of the relationship in its reciprocity. It nevertheless constitutes a constraint which, in tandem with the constraints imposed by social structures, stands in the way of real productivity. We cannot but admire scythes, baskets, pitchers or ploughs, amalgams of gestures and forces, of symbols and functions, decorated and stylized by human energy and shaped by the forms of the human body, by the exertions they imply and by the matter they transform; yet the magnificence of such conformities remains subordinate to the limitations of the relationship in question. Man is not free with respect to these objects, nor are these objects free with respect to man. A revolution in energy sources had to occur – long-range practical control had to become possible, along with the storage and measurement of a newly mobile energy – before man and object could be drawn into a fresh, objective dialogue, into a conflict-laden dialectic which had never been implicit in the reciprocal goal-directedness of their former constrained relationship. Only then could man embark upon an objective process of social development and the object likewise tend in the direction of its own truth, that is, its functionality multiplied by the amount of energy released.

For the real object is the functional object. Revolutions in the field of energy entail the replacement of energy symbiosis and symbolic compliance by the rationality of technology and the (relative) rationality of the reign of production. By the same token, man's relationship to objects becomes subject to a social dialectic which is basically that of the forces of production. What interests us here, however, is the impact of this upheaval on the realm of everyday life.

The Functional Gestural System: Control
We know from our practical experience how very far the mediation of gestures between man and things has been stretched:

household appliances, cars, gadgetry, heating, lighting, communications and transportation systems – all require no more than
minimal energy and action in order to function properly. Often a
slight motion of hand or eye suffices; no dexterity is called for – at
the most, reflexes. The domestic world, almost as much as the
world of work, is governed by regular gestures of control and
remote control. Buttons, levers, handles, pedals (even nothing at
all – as when one passes in front of a photo-electric cell) have thus
replaced pressure, percussion, impact or balance achieved by
means of the body, the intensity and distribution of force, and
the abilities of the hand (from which little more than quickness is
now asked). A prehension of objects involving the whole body has
given way to simple contact (of hand or foot) and simple
surveillance (by the eye or, occasionally, by the ear). In other
words, only man's 'extremities' now have an active part to play in
the functional environment.

The liberating abstractness of energy sources is thus accompanied
by a concomitant abstractness of human praxis with respect to
objects. What is called for here is less a neuromuscular praxis than
what Pierre Naville describes as a system of cerebro-sensory vigi-
lance. But such a system cannot be self-sufficient: the total abstractness of remote action must be mitigated by what I refer to as a
gestural system of control (by hand, eye, etc.).[28] There is a sense in
which this minimal gestural system is essential, for without it all this
abstract power would become meaningless. Man has to be reassured

28. To be more exact, it is not simply that the old gestural system of effort
has been stretched out into a gestural system of control: it has also been split
into a gestural system of control and a gestural system of *play*. Ignored by
modern praxis, but nonetheless freed from its old constraints, the body finds
genuine expression in sports and physical leisure activities – or at any rate,
these supply it with a compensatory release, for we may well ask whether the
splitting into two of the gestural system of effort institutes any real freedom
of the body, or whether it merely establishes a binomial whose second term
(in this case, games and sports) does no more than compensate for the first. A
parallel might be drawn here with the splitting of time into active time and
leisure time.

about his power by some sense of participation, albeit a merely formal one. So the gestural system of control must be deemed indispensable – not to make the system work *technically*, for more advanced technology could (and no doubt will) make it unnecessary, but, rather, to make that system work *psychologically*.

A New Operational Field

Since the energy of objects is abstract, their functionality is limitless: just as there is now scarcely any substance that has no plastic equivalent, so there is no gesture that cannot be replaced by technology. The simplest of mechanisms is liable to replace and subsume a whole set of gestures, concentrating their effectiveness and becoming independent not only of the agent but also of the material acted upon. Form and utility of the tool, raw material, energy applied – all these factors have changed. Thus the matter dealt with has undergone infinite differentiation – even to the point of disappearing altogether: that processed by a radio, for example, is information. The transformation of energy has entailed that of both materials and functions, for technology is not content merely to encapsulate earlier gestures, it also invents new operations, and above all splits up the operational field into completely different functions or sets of functions. Man's abstract relationship to his (technical) objects, his 'spectacular alienation', is thus less a matter of his gestures having been *replaced* than of the abstractness of the very way in which functions have been *split up*, and the impossibility of any analogical apprehension of this splitting-up by reference to earlier gestures.[29] Only an abstract

29. The fire is a case in point. Originally the 'hearth' filled the combined functions of heating, cooking and lighting. This was the basis of its symbolic complexity. Later, the kitchen stove – already a kind of appliance – took over the functions of heating and cooking, while retaining a certain symbolic presence. Eventually all three tasks were separated in analytic fashion and assigned to separate specialized appliances whose synthetic aspect lay not in the concrete unity of the hearth but solely in the abstract identity of the energy (gas or electricity) on which they ran. This new environment, based on a completely different division of functions, has no symbolic dimension whatsoever.

(never an unmediated) intelligence can adapt to the new technical structures; meanwhile, man himself has yet to adapt to the increasingly exclusive use of these higher functions of intelligence and calculation. Resistance here has deep roots, and creates an irreparable delay. Man has become less rational than his own objects, which now run ahead of him, so to speak, organizing his surroundings and thus appropriating his actions. Take the washing machine, for instance. In its form and operation it has no clear relationship to the clothes washed. The whole operation of washing has lost its specificity in space and time; it is a minimal intervention, a timed procedure in which the water itself is no more than an abstract vehicle for detergent chemicals. Functionally speaking, the washing machine belongs, therefore, to a relational field utterly different from that of the old-fashioned washboard or washtub – a functional field of associations which is no longer coextensive with other objective operations, with the refrigerator, with the television, with the components of interior design, or with the automobile. Traditional tools, by contrast, belonged to a field of practical mediation between the material to be transformed and the person doing the transforming. We have thus moved from the depth of a vertical field to the extension of a horizontal one.

Just as the various parts of an object's mechanism have structure, so the various technical objects tend, independently of man, to become organized by themselves, to refer to one another in the uniformity of their simplified praxis, and thus come to constitute an articulated order, pursuing its own mode of technological development, wherein man's role does not go beyond a mechanical control which may well ultimately be taken over by the machine itself.

Miniaturization

In place of the continuous (but finite) *space* that gestures create for their purposes around the traditional object, the technical object institutes discontinuous and unlimited *extension*. The principle that regulates this new extension, this functional dimension, is the requirement that organization be maximized and communication optimized. Consequently, technological progress is now accompanied by an ever stronger tendency towards the miniaturization of technical objects.

Freed now from the need to refer to the human scale, to the 'life-size', and ever more taken up by the complexity of messages, mechanisms tend increasingly, on the model of the brain, towards an irreversible concentration of their structures, towards the quintessentially microcosmic.[30] After the Promethean expansion of a technology striving to occupy the whole world, the entirety of space, we are now entering the era of a technology that works on the world 'in depth', so to speak. The reign of electronics and cybernetics means that efficiency, freed from the shackles of gestural space, is henceforward dependent upon a saturation of minimal extension, governing a maximized field, which is without common measure with sensory experience.[31]

30. This is the reason for our fascination with miniaturized watches, transistor radios, cameras, and so forth.

31. This tendency to miniaturize may seem paradoxical in the context of a civilization of extension, expansion and spatialization. It is a tendency, however, that embodies both the ideal goal of that civilization and a contradiction within it. For our technological civilization is also a civilization of limits imposed on urban life, of a critical scarcity of space. And it is increasingly, by absolute everyday necessity (and not just by structural necessity), a civilization of the 'compact'. There is undoubtedly a link between lasers, calculators and microtechnology on the one hand and small cars, multifunctional gadgets, 'planned' flats and transistor radios on the other – but this link is not necessarily structural or logical. The principle of maximum organization which gives rise to technologies of miniaturization has the parallel function of palliating (though not resolving) a chronic shortage of space in everyday life. The two functions are not structurally related; it is simply that both are bound up with each other in the context of a single system. As for the everyday technical object, caught between the two, it is uncertain whether it represents a technological advance (miniaturization) or a degrading of the practical system (shortage of space). (The antagonism between structural technological evolution and the constraints of scarcity which govern the system as directly experienced is discussed later – see 'The Transformations of Technology', pp. 123 ff. below.)

Stylization, Manipulability, Envelopment

The stylization of forms is invariably a corollary of the growing autonomy of the functional world and the optimized organization of space in its extension. Forms themselves also become more autonomous as they diverge further and further from a morphology founded on the human body and on the physical effort exerted by that body, yet they continue to allude thereto in one way or another. They organize themselves independently, but their former relationship to primary functions subsists in the abstractness of the sign: this is their *connotation*. Consider the hand, whose importance for the gestural system of control we have already mentioned. The first aim of all modern objects is manipulability ('manipulable' being virtually synonymous with 'functional'). But just what is the nature of the 'hand' which thus determines the forms of these objects? Certainly no longer the prehensile organ that focuses effort: rather, nothing more than the abstract *sign* of manipulability, to which buttons, handles, and so on are all the better suited in that the operation concerned no longer calls for manual labour and, indeed, takes place elsewhere. Here we rediscover (though now on the morphological plane) the myth of naturalness of which we spoke above: the human body delegates no more than the signs of its presence to objects whose functioning, in any case, is independent from now on. At the very most it delegates its 'extremities', while objects, for their part, are 'contoured' in accordance with an abstract morphological meaning. There is a collusion of forms here which no longer refers to man save by way of allusion.[32] It is in this sense only that the object's form 'weds' the hand, that Airborne's armchair (of which more later) 'weds' the shape of your body: one form adapts to another. The traditional object or tool, by contrast, was not in any way 'wedded' to human forms; what it wedded was human physical

32. Just as we saw that in the realm of atmosphere, nature is no more than an allusion.

effort and human gestures – indeed, the human body imposed itself upon that tool in order to carry out a material task. Today the human body would seem to be present only as the abstract justification for the finished form of the functional object. *Functionality is thus no longer the imposition of a real task, but simply the adaptation of one form to another (as of handle to hand) and the consequent supersession or omission of the actual processes of work.*

Thus freed from practical functions and from the human gestural system, forms become purely relative with respect both to one another and to the space to which they lend 'rhythm'. This is how we now define the 'style' of objects: inasmuch as their mechanism is virtual or taken for granted (a few simple gestures evoke its power without making it manifest, while the effective physical embodiment of the object remains indecipherable), it is only their form which is present – which wraps that mechanism in its perfection and confines it within its contours, cloaking and eliminating an energy that has been made into an abstraction and, as it were, crystallized. As in the development of some animal species, the form is externalized, enclosing the object in a sort of carapace. Fluid, transitive, enveloping, it unifies appearances by transcending the alarming discontinuity of the various mechanisms involved and replacing it with a coherent whole. A functional atmosphere implies a continuous closure of line (also of material – of chrome, enamel or plastic) which restores the unity of a world whose profound equilibrium was formerly guaranteed by human gestures. We are heading towards an absolutism of forms: only the form is called for, only the form is read, and at the deepest level it is the functionality of forms that defines 'style'.

The End of the Symbolic Dimension
The fact is that this formal achievement papers over an essential lack; our technological civilization tries to use the universal transitivity of form as a means of compensating for the disappearance of the symbolic relationship associated with the tradi-

tional gestural system of work, as a way of making up for the unreality, the symbolic void, of our power.[33]

For gestural mediation is by no means confined to the practical realm, and the energy invested in physical effort is not merely muscular and nervous. Gestures and physical effort are also the vectors of a whole phallic symbolism, as deployed, for example, in such notions as penetration, resistance, moulding or rubbing. The rhythm of the sexual act is the prototype of all rhythmical gestures, and all technological praxis is overdetermined by it.[34] Because they press the whole body into the service of effort and accomplishment, traditional objects and tools acquire something of the deep libidinal cathexis of sexual exchange (as, at another level, do dance and ritual).[35] But of course all this is discouraged, demobilized, by the advent of the technical object. Everything once sublimated – and hence cathected symbolically – in the gestural system of work is now repressed. No vestige remains in our technical utilities of the theatrical and anarchic outgrowths of the objects of earlier

33. The last thing I want to do, however, is romanticize either physical labour or the traditional gestural system. When one contemplates the centuries during which man was obliged to make up with his own strength for the shortcomings of his tools, when one recalls that, long after the day of slaves and serfs, peasants and craftsmen continued to manipulate objects unchanged since the Stone Age, one can only applaud the new abstractness of energy sources and the decline of a gestural system which was, after all, an appurtenance of servitude. The 'soulless machinism' of today – down to and including electric potato-mashers – is what has made it possible to get beyond the strict equivalence of gesture and product which once used up every moment of every endless day: at long last human gestures can embody a *surplus*. The consequences on another level, however, are nonetheless very far-reaching.
34. See Gaston Bachelard and Gilbert Durand, *Les structures anthropologiques de l'Imaginaire* (second edition, Paris: Presses Universitaires de France, 1963).
35. Similarly, it is arguable that the gestural system also facilitates the integration into objects of what Piaget calls paternal and maternal 'affective schemata' – the child's relationships to its primal human milieu: the father and mother themselves appear to the child as tools surrounded by other, secondary, tools.

times, which showed their age, and made no secret of the work they did. Spades and pitchers were living phalluses or vaginas in whose 'obscenity' the instinctual dynamics of human beings lay open to a symbolic reading.[36] The whole gestural system of work was also obscene, in sharp contrast to the miniaturized and abstract gestural system of control to which it has now been reduced. The world of the objects of old seems like a theatre of cruelty and instinctual drives in comparison with the formal neutrality and prophylactic 'whiteness' of our perfect functional objects. Thus the handle of the flatiron gradually diminishes as it undergoes 'contouring' – the term is typical in its superficiality and abstractness; increasingly it suggests the very absence of gesture, and carried to its logical extreme this handle will no longer be manual – merely manipulable. At that point, *the perfecting of the form will have relegated man to a pure contemplation of his power.*

The Abstractness of Power

Man's technical power can thus no longer be mediated, for it has no common measure with the human being and the human body. Nor, by extension, can it any longer be *symbolized*: functional forms can do no more than *connote* it. Certainly they overburden it with meaning in their absolute consistency (aerodynamism, manipulability, automaticity, etc.), but at the same time they are formal expressions of the void that separates us from our power; in a sense they are the ritual that accompanies the miracle-working of the modern world. They are the signs of our power, then, but also testimony to our irresponsibility with respect to that power. It is

36. Thus the classic maternal house of children's drawings, with its doors and windows, symbolizes both the child itself (a human face) and the body of the mother. Like the disappearance of the old gestural system, the disappearance of this traditional house, complete with storeys, staircase, attic and cellar, signals first and foremost the frustration of a faculty of symbolic recognition: the modern order disappoints us because it stymies any profound involvement, any visceral perception of our own body; because we can now recognize therein scarcely any aspect of our bodily organs, of our somatic organization.

here, perhaps, that we should seek the reason for the morose technical satisfaction to which initial euphoria over mechanical achievement has so quickly given way, for the peculiar anxiety that takes hold of all beneficiaries of the wonders of the object, of obligatory non-involvement, and of the passively observed spectacle of their own power. The uselessness of habitual gestures and the breakdown of everyday routines founded on movements of the body have a profound psychophysiological impact. Indeed, a genuine revolution has taken place on the everyday plane: *objects have now become more complex than human behaviour relative to them.* Objects are more and more highly differentiated – our gestures less and less so. To put it another way: objects are no longer surrounded by the theatre of gesture in which they used to be simply the various roles; instead their emphatic goal-directedness has very nearly turned them into the actors in a global process in which *man* is merely the role, or the spectator.

There is a moral to be drawn from the following little tale. We are in the eighteenth century. An illusionist well versed in clockwork has devised an automaton. An automaton so perfect, with movements so fluid and natural, that when the illusionist and his creation appear on the stage together, the audience cannot tell which is which. The illusionist then finds himself obliged to make his own gestures mechanical, and – in what is really the pinnacle of his art – to alter his own appearance slightly so as to give his show its full meaning; the spectators would eventually chafe if they were left in doubt as to which of the two figures was 'real', and the neatest solution is that they should take the man for the machine, and vice versa. . . .

This story provides a good illustration of a familiar fatal relationship to technology, even though in the case of modern reality we do not awake to the applause of an audience delighted to have been so thoroughly duped; a good analogy for a society with a technical apparatus so highly perfected that it appears to be a 'synthetic' gestural system superior to the traditional system, a sovereign projection of fully realized mental structures. For the time being the human gesture is still alone capable of supplying the precision and flexibility demanded by certain tasks, but there is no reason to assume that the unceasing forward march of *techne* will not eventually achieve a mimesis which replaces a natural world with an intelligible artificial one. If the simulacrum is so well designed that it becomes an effective organizer of reality, then surely it is man, not the simulacrum, who is turned into an abstraction. It was already apparent to Lewis Mumford that 'the machine leads to a lapse of function which is but one step away from paralysis'.[37] This is no longer a mechanistic hypothesis but reality as directly experienced: the behaviour that technical objects impose is a broken-up sequence of impoverished gestures, of sign-gestures bereft of rhythm. It is rather like what happens to the illusionist of the story who, in response to the perfection of his machine, is led to dismantle and mechanize himself. *The coherence of his own structural projection thus relegates man to the inchoate.* In the face of the functional object the human being becomes dysfunctional, irrational and subjective: an empty form, open therefore to the mythology of the functional, to projected phantasies stemming from the stupefying efficiency of the outside world.

The Functionalist Myth

For the concrete dynamic of effort has not disappeared completely into the abstraction of the mechanisms and gestures of control. It has been internalized as the mental dynamic of a functionalist myth: the myth of the possibility of a totally functional world of which every present-day technical object is already a sign. The repressed gestural system is thus transformed into myth, projection, transcendence. No sooner do we lose sight of the route taken by energy, feel energy to be intrinsic to the object, become the

37. *Technics and Civilization* (New York: Harcourt Brace, 1934; reprint, San Diego and New York: Harcourt Brace, 1963), p. 344. Page references are to the reprint edition.

non-responsible beneficiaries of an absence (or nearabsence) of any need for gesture and physical effort, than we are surely justified in believing – indeed, are obliged to believe – in an absolute and limitless functionality, in efficacy as the virtue of signs. Something is revived here of the ancient habit, prevalent in a world of magic, of inferring reality from signs. 'Part of the feeling of the efficacy of primitive magic has survived in the unconditional belief in progress,' writes Gilbert Simondon.[38] This applies not only to technological society in a global sense but also – confusedly but tenaciously – to the everyday environment, where the most insignificant of gadgets may be the focal point of a techno-mythological realm of power. The way objects are used in everyday life implies an almost authoritarian set of assumptions about the world. And what the technical object bespeaks, no longer requiring anything more than our formal participation, is a world without effort, an abstract and completely mobile energy, and the total efficacy of sign-gestures.[39]

Functional Form: The Lighter
All this is exemplified in the stylized fluidity of 'functional' forms. It is precisely this mental dynamic, this simulacrum of a lost symbolic relationship, that such forms connote in their striving to reinvent a teleology from signs alone. Consider the lighter shaped like a pebble which has been successfully promoted by the advertisers in the last few years. Oblong, elliptical and asymmetrical in form, it is described as 'highly functional' – not that it is better than any other lighter for lighting cigarettes, but because it

---

38. *Du mode d'existence des objects techniques* (Paris: Aubier, 1958), p. 95.
39. This *mythology* must be distinguished from the *ideology* of Progress, which, abstract as it may be, is still a hypothesis about structures which is based on actual technological development. The functionalist myth, by contrast, is no more than the presumption, taken on faith from the mere testimony of signs, of the existence of a technological totality. The ideology of Progress is a socio-cultural mediation of the eighteenth and nineteenth centuries; the functionalist myth is an anticipatory fantasy.

is 'perfectly shaped to fit into the palm of the hand'. 'The sea has polished it to the form of the hand': it is in a finished state. Its functionality resides not in its ability to light but in its manipulability. It is as though its form was predisposed by nature (the sea) for manipulation. This new teleonomy constitutes the rhetoric of this object. The connotation here is twofold: though it is an industrial product, this lighter is supposed to have retrieved one of the qualities of the craft object in that its form is an extension of the human gesture and the human body; meanwhile, the allusion to the sea takes us into the realm of a mythical nature itself culturalized as a function of man and perfectly adapted to man's every last desire: the sea plays the cultural role of polisher – an instance of nature's sublime craftsmanship.[40] The action of sea on stone is thus echoed by the hand creating fire; the lighter becomes a miraculous flint, and a prehistoric and craftsmanly purposiveness comes into play in the very practical essence of an industrial object.

Formal Connotation: Tail Fins

There was a long period during which American cars were adorned by immense tail fins. For Vance Packard these perfectly symbolized the American obsession with consumer goods.[41] They have other meanings, too: scarcely had it emancipated itself from the forms of earlier kinds of vehicles than the automobile-object began connoting nothing more than the result so achieved – that is to say, nothing more than itself as a victorious function. We thus witnessed a veritable triumphalism on the part of the object: the car's fins became the sign of victory over space – and they were *purely* a sign, because they bore no direct relationship to that victory (indeed, if anything they ran counter to it, tending as they did to make vehicles both heavier and more cumbersome).

40. Mythologies of the 'natural' generally evoke an earlier cultural system as a kind of pseudo-historical reference-point in their regression to a mythical totality. Thus the mythology of pre-industrial craftsmanship implies the myth of a 'functional' nature, and vice versa.
41. See *The Waste Makers* (New York: David McKay, 1960).

Concrete technical mobility was over-signified here as absolute fluidity. Tail fins were a sign not of *real* speed but of a sublime, measureless speed. They suggested a miraculous automatism, a sort of grace. It was the presence of these fins that in our imagination propelled the car, which, thanks to them, seemed to fly along of its own accord, after the fashion of a higher organism. The engine was the real efficient principle, the fins the imaginary one. Such interplay between the spontaneous and the transcendent efficacy of the object calls immediately for nature symbols: cars sprout fins and are encased in fuselages – features that in other contexts are functional; first they appropriate the characteristics of the aeroplane, which is a model object relative to space, then they proceed to borrow directly from nature – from sharks, birds, and so on.

These days connotations of the natural have shifted to a different register. Formerly we were treated to a flood of motifs from the vegetable kingdom which, as a way of naturalizing them, submerged objects and even machines in signs of the fruits of the earth.[42] Now, by contrast, we are seeing the emergence of a systematization based on fluidity that seeks connotations no longer in earth or flora, which are static elements, but instead in air and water, which are fluid ones, as also in the dynamic world of animals. Despite this shift from organic to fluid, however, the modern version of naturalness does still refer to nature: astructural, inessential features such as the tail fin still lend *natural* connotations to technical objects.

It follows that such connotation is *allegorical* in character. When a fixed structure is invaded by astructural elements, when the object itself is overwhelmed by a formal detail, the true function is no longer anything but a pretext, and *the form does no more than signify the idea of the function.* In other words, the

42. Only curves still retain something of these vegetable and maternal overtones, tending to invest objects with the organic sense of *containing.* The sense, by extension, of natural evolution. They are consequently disappearing or becoming elliptical.

form has become allegorical. Tail fins are our modern allegory. We may have no more muses, no more flowers, but we do have fins on our cars and lighters polished by the sea. It is through allegory, moreover, that the discourse of the unconscious makes itself heard. The deep-rooted phantasy of speed finds expression in tail fins, but it does so in an allusive and regressive manner. For while speed has a phallic character, the speed evoked by tail fins is merely formal, fixed, and, as it were, visually edible. Speed so apprehended is no longer the result of an active process but, rather, the result of pleasure taken in speed-in-effigy, so to speak – the final, passive state of an energy completely degraded to the level of a pure sign, to a level where unconscious desire is forever chewing over an arrested discourse.

Thus formal connotation is indeed tantamount to the imposition of a *censorship*. Behind the functional self-realization of forms, traditional phallic symbolism has fallen apart: on the one hand this system has become abstract, a simulacrum of power (mechanism being concealed or indecipherable); at the same time, regressively and narcissistically, it is content to let itself be enveloped by forms and their 'functionality'.

Form as Camouflage

A clearer picture thus begins to emerge of the way in which forms discourse, and of the orientation of that discourse. Inasmuch as forms are relative to one another, and continually refer to other, homologous forms, they present the aspect of a finished discourse – the optimal realization of an essence of man and an essence of the world. This discourse is never innocent, however: the articulation of forms among themselves always conceals another, indirect discourse. Thus the form of the lighter relates to the form of the hand, but only *by way of* the sea, which 'has polished it'; and a car's tail fins relate to the distance covered only *by way of* the aeroplane, the shark, and so on. More precisely, it is the *idea* of the sea, the aeroplane or the shark that mediates. It is the Idea of Nature which, in its myriad forms (animal or vegetable elements, the human body, space itself[43]), everywhere becomes involved in the articulation of forms. And to the extent that those forms constitute a system and thus re-create a kind of internal purposiveness, their reciprocal connotations are 'natural' – for nature remains the ideal point of reference of all goal-directedness.

'Vulgar' objects – objects that are nothing more than their function – embody no such purposiveness. In their case there is no justification for speaking of 'atmosphere', merely of environment. For a good while attempts were nevertheless made to endow them with a crude purposiveness: sewing machines were decorated with flowers, and it is not so long since Cocteau and Buffet could be found 'dressing up' refrigerators. Alternatively, if it proved impossible to 'naturalize' them, their existence would simply be concealed. After a rather brief period during which machines and technology flaunted their practical nature in obscene fashion out of sheer pride at their recent emancipation, the modesty that now reigns strives vigorously to veil all the practical functions of things. We are told that 'oil heating, once installed, is absolutely invisible'. Or: 'Though it is indispensable, the garage is not supposed to catch the eye from anywhere in the garden. So it has been hidden beneath a rockery. Alpine flowers cover its concrete roof, and access to the main house from the garage is via a little door concealed in the rockery.'

43. The fact is that space itself has the connotation of *emptiness*; instead of space arising from the living interrelationship between forms (as a space with 'rhythms'), forms are apprehended, in their relationship to each other, *by way of* the emptiness which is the formalized sign of space. A room containing space so understood creates a 'natural' effect: we say that it is 'airy'. This is the temptation of emptiness, as when unadorned walls indicate culture and luxury. An *objet d'art* may seem more precious when it is surrounded by empty space. 'Atmosphere' is thus very often created merely by a formal arrangement which 'personalizes' particular objects through the disposition of empty space. In the case of serially produced objects, conversely, a shortage of space destroys atmosphere by depriving objects of the luxury of 'breathing'. (Should we perhaps interpret this affectation of emptiness as an echo of a moral order founded on distinction and distance?) Here too, then, we find that a traditional connotation has been reversed, for fullness and substantiality once served to valorize accumulation and naïve ostentation.

Naturalization, concealment, superimposition, décor – we are surrounded by objects whose form comes into play as *a false answer to the self-contradictory manner in which the object is experienced.* Recently disparities of décor have given way to subtler solutions. The connotation of nature, however, embedded as it is in the very discourse of forms, is still always present.

The naturalizing tendency spontaneously assumes a burden of moral and psychological meanings. Here the lexicon of advertising is telling. In this discourse a whole battery of emotionally laden words such as 'warmth', 'intimacy', 'radiance' and 'honesty' – a whole rhetoric of 'natural' values – goes hand in hand with the careful calculation of forms and the promotion of 'functional style'. All the talk of warmth, honesty or faithfulness bears eloquent witness to the dubiousness of a system in which long-lost traditional values reappear as signs, in exactly the same way as the signs of shark, space or sea appeared in our earlier examples. Clearly one cannot properly speak of 'hypocrisy' here. But surely this systematic, homogeneous and functional world, with its colours, materials and forms, which at every moment, though it does not actually *negate* them, does disavow, deny and omit drives, desires, and all the explosive force of the instinctual life[44] – surely this, too, is a moral – even a hyper-moral – world? Hypocrisy in its modern version consists not in concealing the obscenity of nature but, rather, in *being satisfied (or attempting to be satisfied) by the inoffensive naturalness of signs.*

44. The *moral* refusal of the instinctual itself signals an instinctual pro-miscuity. Here, by contrast, there is no more promiscuity: nature in all its forms is simultaneously signified and disavowed at the actual level of the sign.

III Conclusion: Naturalness and Functionality

It will be clear from the foregoing discussion of the values of interior design and atmosphere that the entire system is founded on the concept of FUNCTIONALITY. Colours, forms, materials, design, space – all are functional. Every object claims to be functional, just as every regime claims to be democratic. The term evokes all the virtues of modernity, yet it is perfectly ambiguous. With its reference to 'function' it suggests that the object fulfils itself in the precision of its relationship to the real world and to human needs. But as our analysis has shown, *'functional' in no way qualifies what is adapted to a goal, merely what is adapted to an order or system*: functionality is the ability to become integrated into an overall scheme. An object's functionality is the very thing that enables it to transcend its main 'function' in the direction of a secondary one, to play a part, to become a combining element, an adjustable item, within a universal system of signs.

The functional system is thus characterized, *in a throughly ambiguous way*, on the one hand by a *transcendence* of the traditional system under its three aspects – as the primary function of the object, as drives and primary needs, and as a set of symbolic relations between the two – and on the other hand by a simultaneous *disavowal* of these three mutually reinforcing aspects of the traditional system. In other words:

1. The coherence of the functional system of objects depends on the fact that these objects – along with their various properties,

such as colour, form, and so on – no longer have any value of their own, but merely a universal value as signs. The order of Nature (primary functions, instinctual drives, symbolic relationships) is everywhere present in the system, but present only as signs. The materiality of objects no longer directly confronts the materiality of needs, these two inconsistent primary and antagonistic systems having been suppressed by the insertion between them of the new, abstract system of manipulable signs – by the insertion, in a word, of *functionality*. At the same stroke the symbolic relationship likewise disappears. What emerges from the realm of signs is a nature continuously dominated, an abstract, worked-upon nature, rescued from time and anxiety, which the sign is constantly converting into culture. This nature has been systematized: it is not so much nature as naturalness (or, equally well, 'cultural-ness'[45]). Such naturalness is thus the corollary of all functionality – and the connotation of the modern system of 'atmosphere'.

2. The always *transcended* presence of Nature (in a far more consistent and exhaustive fashion than in any earlier culture[46]) is

45. For indeed, there is no longer any antagonism here between culture and nature, save in the most formal sense, and the two are exchangeable at the level of signs. When we speak of naturalness [*naturalité*] and 'culturalness' [*culturalité*], the '-ness' is the important thing: the French suffix '*-ité*' always marks the shift to an abstract, secondary meaning operating at the level of signs, as witness *fin/finalité* (goal/teleonomy), *fonction/fonctionalité*, *histoire/historialité* (history/historicalness), *personne/personnalité*, etc. Such words tend, therefore, to have an essential role in the analysis of systematizations, particularly in connection with the structures of connotation. They have thus cropped up a good deal already in our present discussion, and will crop up again later. [*Translator's note*. As may be seen from the author's examples of '*-ité*' words, the cognate suffix '-ity' is not used in a way that would allow this pattern of meaning to be reflected in English translation. '*Culturalité*' has generally been translated as 'cultural connotation'.]

46. For culture, after all, has never been anything else. But today, for the first time, at the level of everyday life, the foundation has been laid for a system whose abstractness makes it capable of completely determining objects, hence of extending its internal autonomy very widely, even to the point (and this is its teleonomy) of achieving a perfect synchrony between man and his surroundings by reducing both to simple signs and elements.

what confers on this system its validity as a cultural model and its objective dynamism. But at the same time the always *denied* presence of Nature makes the system into a system of disavowal, lack, and camouflage (and this, too, in a way far more consistent than in all previous systems).

On the one hand, then, organization and calculation; on the other, connotation and disavowal. Both flow, however, from a single function of the sign, and together they constitute the one and only reality of the functional world.

Addendum: The Domestic World and the Car

The discussion that we have just brought to a close has been confined in its essentials to the domestic environment, to the dwelling-place. The private realm of the household is indeed where the vast majority of our everyday objects are to be found. The *system* nevertheless extends beyond the domestic interior – notably to an external item which itself constitutes an entire dimension of it: the motorcar.

The car epitomizes the object, perfectly illustrating every trait we have described: the rendering abstract of any practical goal in the interests of speed and prestige, formal connotation, technical connotation, forced differentiation, emotional cathexis, and projection in phantasy. Here more easily than anywhere else we may discern the collusion between the subjective system of needs and the objective system of production. I shall return to these points later. For the moment I want to emphasize the importance of the car's place within the system as a whole.

The automobile is a complement to all other objects considered together; each of these in its particularity appears merely partial in comparison with the automobile – not only because it is less complex, but also because it does not occupy its own specific position in the system. Only the domestic sphere *as a whole* (furniture, appliances, gadgets, etc.), as structured by the major distinction between interior design and atmosphere, holds a position comparable in value, in its relative coherence, to that of the car. True, at the level of lived experience the domestic realm, with its multiplicity of tasks, functions and relationships, is far more significant than the 'realm' of car-related activity. Yet it is undeniable that at the level of the *system* it no longer constitutes anything more than one binary pole of the global system, the other being cars.

Travel is a necessity, and speed is a pleasure. Possession of a car implies more: the driving licence is a sort of passport, a letter of credit from an aristocracy whose domain is the very latest in engine compression and speed. Disqualification from driving is surely tantamount to an excommunication, to a kind of social castration.[47]

Without going so far as to treat the car as a modern version of the old centaurian myth of a fusion between human intelligence and animal strength,[48] one may certainly describe it as a sublime object, for it opens a parenthesis, as it were, in the everydayness of all other objects. The material that it transforms, namely space-time, cannot be compared to any other. And the dynamic synthesis of space-time that the car offers in the shape of speed is likewise radically distinct from any kind of normal function. Movement alone is the basis of a sort of happiness, but the mechanical euphoria associated with speed is something else altogether, grounded for the imagination in the miracle of motion. Effortless mobility entails a kind of pleasure that is unrealistic, a kind of suspension of existence, a kind of absence of responsibility. The effect of speed's integration of space-time is to reduce the world to two-dimensionality, to an image, stripping away its relief and its historicity and in a way ushering one into a state of sublime immobility and contemplation. 'Movement', says Schelling, 'is merely the search for repose.' Beyond a hundred kilometres per

47. It has occasionally been used as a penalty for procurers.
48. On centaur mythology and phantasy projections onto horses and cars, see the discussion of 'Collecting' below.

hour there is a presumption of eternity (as also, perhaps, of neurosis . . .). Security founded on the sense of a world beyond or a world prior to this one is what nourishes car-induced euphoria, which has nothing of an active tonicity about it; rather, it is a passive satisfaction, albeit one accompanied by ever-changing scenery.

This 'dynamic euphoria' serves as an antithesis to the static joys of family life and immovable property, and opens a parenthesis in social reality. Chris Marker's film *Le joli mai* presents the confession of one person among millions of others for whom the automobile represents a kind of no-man's-land between workplace and family home, an empty vector of pure transport: 'I have no more good moments,' he says, 'except for those I spend between my house and my office. I drive, I drive. These days, though, I am not happy even then, because there is too much traffic.' It is not simply that the car rivals the house as an alternative zone of everyday life: the car, too, is an abode, but an exceptional one; it is a closed realm of intimacy, but one released from the constraints that usually apply to the intimacy of home, one endowed with a formal freedom of great intensity and a dizzying functionality. Home means a regressive attachment to domestic relationships and habits, whereas the intimacy of the car arises from an accelerated space-time metabolism and, inextricably, from the fact that the car may at any time become the locus of an *accident*: the culmination in a chance event – which may in fact never occur but is always imagined, always involuntarily assumed to be inevitable – of that intimacy with oneself, that formal liberty, which is never so beautiful as in death. The car achieves an extraordinary compromise, for it makes it possible to be simultaneously at home and further and further away from home. It is thus the centre of a new kind of subjectivity, but a centre bounded by no circumference, whereas the subjectivity of the domestic world is strictly circumscribed.

No other everyday object, gadget or appliance offers a sublimation or transfiguration of this order. Every functional object is overdetermined in its power, but such overdetermination is minimal in the spheres of household management and home ownership. Moreover, the house as a whole, except to the extent that it achieves self-transcendence by virtue of status or fashion, is not a recipient or bestower of value. (In fact a basic problem for couples is the common failure of the home to catalyse any such reciprocal valorization.) As opposed to the 'horizontal' sector of everyday domestic life, cars and their speed represent a sort of 'vertical' scheme, a sort of third dimension.[49] An 'aristocratic' dimension, too, in that it is free not only from the organic constraints of existence but also from social constraints. Whereas the domestic world seems to fall back to a place on the hither side of the social, cars, with their pure functionality which depends solely on the mastery of space and time, appear to deploy their virtues somewhere *beyond* society. Indeed, relative to the social sphere, household and motorcar partake of the same *private* abstractness, and the binomial they thus constitute, when it is articulated with another, that of work and leisure, frames the entirety of everyday experience.

This systematic bipolarity (the car as eccentric relative to the household yet at the same time complementary to it) tends to map onto the sociological distribution of sex roles. Very often the car remains a male preserve. 'Daddy has HIS Peugeot,' runs one advertising slogan, 'and Mummy has HER Peugeots': the father gets the Peugeot car and the mother gets the Peugeot egg-beater, the Peugeot coffee mill and the Peugeot electric mixer.[50] The family universe is a universe of foods and multifunctional appliances; as for the man, he rules over the world outside, the effective sign of which is the automobile: he himself does not appear in the picture. The same distinction thus applies both at the level of

49. Hence the familiar reticence of the average motorist with respect to car safety devices such as belts. Safety at home is fine, but the car is from this point of view something quite different – the *opposite* of home, in fact.
50. Admittedly this man-car, woman-house correlation is tending to become weaker, in reality if not at the level of representation.

objects and at the level of roles (and in the Peugeot world, significantly enough, both levels are in evidence).

This parallelism could scarcely be accidental, and indeed it corresponds to profound psychosexual determinations.

We have noted that speed is at once transcendent and intimate. It implies the mastery of space *qua* abstract sign of the real world, and the exercise of this mastery involves narcissistic projection. Think of the 'erotic' significance of the car and of speed: by lifting social taboos and at the same time releasing us from immediate responsibility, the mobility of the car removes a whole set of resistances concerning ourselves and others: dynamism, brio, infatuation, daring – all flow from the freedom of the driver's situation, a situation which also fosters the erotic relationship by bringing into play a dual narcissistic projection onto a single phallic object (the car) or a single objectified phallic function (speed). The eroticism of the car is therefore not that of an active sexual approach but, rather, the passive eroticism of narcissistic seductiveness in both partners, or of a shared narcissistic communion in the same object.[51] The erotic significance of the object here plays the same role as the image (real or mental) in masturbation.

From this perspective it would clearly be wrong to see the motorcar as a woman-object.[52] The fact that advertising always in effect does so, describing cars as compliant, racy, comfortable, practical, obedient, hot, and so on, is a symptom of the general tendency to feminize objects, the woman-object being the adver-

51. A glimpse of this relationship of narcissistic complicity established through an object or a system of objects has recently been offered, apropos of couples, in Georges Perec's novel *Les choses, une histoire des années soixante* (Paris: Julliard, 1965) [English translation by Helen R. Lane: *Things: A Story of the Sixties* (New York: Grove Press, 1967]. No doubt this is a normal feature of modern living-together: everything now conspires to make objects into the fodder of relationships, and relationships themselves (whether sexual, marital, familial or microsocial) into a mere framework for the consumption of objects.

52. Some languages make it masculine, others feminine.

tising world's most effective persuasive device and social myth. All objects, cars included, become women in order to be bought – but this is a function of the cultural system. The profound transformation of the car in phantasy is a different phenomenon altogether. Depending on the way it is used and its particular features (from the racing 'spider' to the luxurious limousine), the motorcar may equally well be invested either with the meaning of power or with the meaning of refuge: it may be a projectile or a dwelling-place. But basically, like all functional mechanical objects, it is experienced – and by everyone, men, women and children – as a phallus, as an object of manipulation, care, and fascination. The car is a projection both phallic and narcissistic, a force transfixed by its own image. We saw above, in connection with tail fins, how the car's very forms connote this unconscious discourse.

B. The Non-Functional System, or Subjective Discourse

I Marginal Objects: Antiques

There is a whole range of objects – including unique, baroque, folkloric, exotic and antique objects – that seem to fall outside the system we have been examining. They appear to run counter to the requirements of functional calculation, and answer to other kinds of demands such as witness, memory, nostalgia or escapism. It is tempting to treat them as survivals from the traditional, symbolic order. Yet for all their distinctiveness, these objects do play a part in modernity, and that is what gives them a double meaning.

Atmospheric Value: Historicalness

The fact is that the marginal object is not an anomaly relative to the system, for *the functionality of modern objects becomes historicalness in the case of the antique object* (or marginality in the baroque object, or exoticism in the primitive object) *without this implying that the object ceases to function as a sign within the system.* What we have here is the connotation of nature, of 'naturalness' – indeed, fundamentally we have the ultimate instantiation of that connotation, which is to be found in signs of previous cultural systems. The cigarette lighter described above had a mythological dimension in its reference to the sea, but it still served a purpose; the way in which antiques refer to the past gives them an *exclusively* mythological character. The antique object no longer has any practical application, its role being merely to *signify*. It is astructural, it refuses structure, it is the extreme case of disavowal of the primary functions. Yet it is not afunctional, nor purely 'decorative', for it has a very specific function within the system, namely the signifying of time.[1]

The system of atmosphere is defined in terms of extension, yet inasmuch as it aspires to be total it must conquer all of existence, including, therefore, the essential dimension of time. Clearly it is not real time but the signs or indices of time that antiques embody.[2] This allegorical presence in no way contradicts the general scheme: nature, time – nothing can escape, and everything is worked out on the level of signs. Time, however, is far less amenable than nature to abstraction and systematization. The living contradiction it enshrines resists integration into the logic of a system. This 'chronic' difficulty is what we see reflected in the spectacular connotation of the antique object. The connotation of naturalness can be subtle, but the connotation of historicalness is always glaring. The immobility of antiques has something self-conscious about it. No matter how fine it is, an antique is always eccentric; no matter how authentic it is, there is always something false about it. And indeed, it *is* false in so far as *it puts itself forward as authentic within a system whose basic principle is by no means authenticity but, rather, the calculation of relationships and the abstractness of signs.*

Symbolic Value: The Myth of the Origin

The antique thus has a particular status. To the extent that it is there to conjure up time as part of the atmosphere, and to the extent that it is experienced as a sign, it is simply one element

1. I am restricting my account to antiques because they are the clearest example of 'non-systematic' objects. Obviously this account might be applied equally well, using the same premises, to other varieties of marginal objects.
2. Just as naturalness is basically a disavowal of nature, so historicalness is a refusal of history masked by an exaltation of the signs of history: history simultaneously invoked and denied.

among others, and relative to all others.[3] On the other hand, to the extent that it is not on a par with other objects and manifests itself as total, as an authentic presence, it enjoys a special psychological standing. It is in this respect that the antique may be said, though it serves no obvious purpose, to serve a purpose nevertheless at a deeper level. What lies behind the persistent search for old things – for antique furniture, authenticity, period style, rusticity, crafts-manship, hand-made products, native pottery, folklore, and so on? What is the reason for the strange acculturation phenomenon whereby advanced peoples seek out signs extrinsic to their own time or space, and increasingly remote relative to their own cultural system (a phenomenon which is the converse of 'under-developed' peoples' attraction to the technological products and signs of the industrialized world)?

The demand to which antiques respond is the demand for definitive or fully realized being.[4] The tense of the mythological object is the perfect: it is that which occurs in the present as having occurred in a former time, hence that which is founded upon itself, that which is 'authentic'. The antique is always, in the strongest sense of the term, a 'family portrait': the immemorialization, in the concrete form of an object, of a former being – a procedure equivalent, in the register of the imaginary, to a suppression of time. This characteristic of antiques is, of course, precisely what is lacking in functional objects, which exist only in the present, in the indicative or in the practical imperative, which exhaust their

3. In point of fact the antique may be perfectly integrated into structures of atmosphere, for its presence is apprehended *en bloc* as 'warm', in contrast to the modern environment as a whole, which is 'cold'.

4. And once again my remarks should be taken as equally applicable, by extension, to exotic objects; for modern man, in any case, changing country or latitude is essentially equivalent to plunging into the past (as tourism well demonstrates). The fascination for hand-made or native products, for bazaar items from all over the globe, arises less from their picturesque variety than from the anteriority of their forms or their manufacture, and from the allusion they contain to an earlier world – invariably a throwback to the world of our childhood and its playthings.

possibilities in use, never having occurred in a former time, and which, though they can in varying degrees support the spatial environment, cannot support the temporal one. The functional object is efficient; the mythological object is fully realized. The fully realized event that the mythological object signifies is birth. I am not the one who *is*, in the present, full of *angst* – rather, I am the one who *has been*, as indicated by the course of the reverse birth of which the antique object is the sign, a course which leads from the present far back into time: a regression, therefore.[5] The antique object thus presents itself as a myth of origins.

'Authenticity'

It is impossible not to draw a comparison between the taste for antiques and the passion for collecting (which we shall be discussing below). There are profound affinities between the two, and in both we find the same narcissistic regression, the same way of suppressing time, the same imaginary mastery of birth and death. All the same, there are two distinctive features of the mythology of the antique object that need to be pointed out: the nostalgia for origins and the obsession with authenticity. It seems to me that both arise from the mythical evocation of birth which the antique object constitutes in its temporal closure – being born implying, after all, that one has had a father and a mother. Obviously, beating a path back to the origins means regression to the mother; the older the object, the closer it brings us to an earlier age, to 'divinity', to nature, to primitive knowledge, and so forth. According to Maurice Rheims, this kind of mystique already existed in the High Middle Ages, when a Greek bronze or intaglio covered with pagan markings could acquire magical virtues in the eyes of a

5. Two opposed tendencies are involved here. Inasmuch as the antique is integrated into the *current* cultural system, it comes from the depths of time *as signifier in the present of the empty dimension of time.* By contrast, the individual regression that the antique object makes possible is *a movement of the present into the past, into which it projects the empty dimension of being.*

ninth-century Christian. The demand for authenticity is, strictly speaking, a very different matter. It is reflected in an obsession with certainty – specifically, certainty as to the origin, date, author and signature of a work. The mere fact that a particular object has belonged to a famous or powerful individual may confer value on it. The fascination of handicraft derives from an object's having passed through the hands of someone the marks of whose labour are still inscribed thereupon: we are fascinated by what has been *created*, and is therefore unique, because the *moment* of creation cannot be reproduced. Now, the search for the *traces of creation*, from the actual impression of the hand to the signature, is also a search for a line of descent and for paternal transcendence. Authenticity always stems from the Father: the Father is the source of value here. And it is this sublime link that antiques evoke in the imagination, along with the return journey to the mother's breast.

The Neo-Cultural Syndrome: Restoration

The quest for *authenticity* (being-founded-on-itself) is thus very precisely a quest for an *alibi* (being-elsewhere). Let me try to shed some light on these two notions by considering a well-known example of nostalgic restoration, as described in an article entitled 'How to Fix Up Your Ruin'.[6] This is what an architect does with an old farm in 'Ile-de-France'[7] that he has taken over and decided to restore:

The walls, crumbling because of the lack of foundations, were demolished. Part of the original barn at the south gable was

6. 'Comment bricoler votre ruine', *La maison française*, May 1963.
7. [*Translator's note*: The author's inverted commas suggest the quaintness of the name 'Ile-de-France' at the time of writing, for this was then an archaic regional denomination with no modern administrative meaning. This changed in 1976, when the entity known as the Région Parisienne was rebaptized Ile-de-France.]

removed to make way for a terrace. . . . Of course the three major walls were reconstructed. For the purposes of water-proofing we left a 0.7-metre space beneath tarred flagstones at ground level. . . . Neither the staircase nor the chimney was part of the original structure. . . . We brought in Marseilles tile, Clamart flags, Burgundian *tuiles* for the roof; we built a garage in the garden and installed large French windows. . . . The kitchen is a hundred per cent modern, as is the bathroom. . . .

HOWEVER: 'The half-timbering, which was in good condition, has been retained in the new construction'; AND: 'The stone frame-work of the main entrance was carefully preserved during demoli-tion, and its stones and tiles were reused.' The article is accompanied by photographs which indeed clearly show just what is left from the old farm in the wake of 'the architect's soundings and categorical choices': three beams and two stone blocks. But on this rock would our architect build his country house – and indeed, the couple of original stones left in that entrance-way now constitute the most fitting of symbolic foundations, reinvesting the whole edifice with value. It is they which exculpate the whole enterprise from all the compromises struck by modernity with nature in order to make the place more comfortable (an innocent enough intention in itself). The architect, now transformed into a gentleman farmer, has in actuality built himself the modern house that he wanted all along, but modernity of itself could not invest the place with value, could not make the house into a 'dwelling-place': true *being* was still lacking. Rather as a church does not become a genuinely sacred place until a few bones or relics have been enshrined in it, so this architect cannot feel at home (in the strongest sense: he cannot thoroughly rid himself of a particular kind of anxiety) until he can sense the infinitesimal yet sublime presence within his brand-new walls of an old stone that bears witness to past generations. Were it not for such witnesses, the oil heating and the garage (surmounted by its Alpine garden!) would be nothing more, sad to say, than what they are – the sad necessities of comfort. Nor is it only the functional arrangements that are exonerated by the authenticity of those old stones, but in some measure also the cultural exoticism of less important decorative elements (which are, naturally, 'in the best of taste and not in the least rustic'): opalescent lamps, straw-bottomed designer armchairs, a Dalmatian chair 'once strapped to the back of a donkey', a Romantic mirror, and so forth. The cunning of the cultural guilty conscience even leads to a curious paradox, for while the garage is concealed by a fake Alpine garden, a warming-pan introduced as a rustic accessory is described as 'there not as part of the décor but as a serviceable utensil'. 'It is used', we are assured, 'in wintertime'! So the garage's practical materiality is masked, but the warming-pan's practical essence is retrieved by means of mental acrobatics. In an oil-heated house a warming-pan is obviously quite superfluous. Yet if it is not used it will no longer be authentic, will become a mere cultural sign: the cultural, purposeless warming-pan will emerge as an all-too-faithful image of the vanity of the attempt to retrieve a natural state of affairs by rebuilding this house – and, indeed, an all-too-faithful image of the architect himself, who, fundamentally, has no part to play here, for his entire social existence lies elsewhere; his very *being* is elsewhere, and for him nature is nothing but a cultural luxury. Which is fair enough, so long as one can afford it. The architect, however, does not see things in that light: if the warming-pan serves no purpose, it is merely a sign of wealth, and is thus of the order of *having*, of status, and not of the order of *being*. It must therefore be declared to have some purpose, in contrast to such truly useful objects as the oil heater and the garage, which are studiously camouflaged, as though they were ineradicable blots on nature. The warming-pan is therefore genuinely mythological; so, for that matter, is the whole house (although in another sense it is totally real and functional, responding as it does to a perfectly clear desire for comfort and fresh air). By choosing not to raze the old farm and build on the site in accordance simply with his own need for comfort, by his insistence on saving old stones and beams, our architect betrays the fact that he experiences the refinement and flawless functionality of his house as inauthentic, that these characteristics do not satisfy his deepest wishes.

Man is not 'at home' amid pure functionality – he requires something like that lustre of the wood of the True Cross which could make a church truly holy, some kind of talisman – a shard of absolute reality ensconced, enshrined at the heart of ordinary reality in order to justify it. Such is the role of the antique object, which always takes on the meaning, in the context of the human environment, of an embryo or mother-cell. By means of such objects a dispersed being identifies with the original and ideal situation of the embryo, retrogressing to the microcosmic yet essential state of prenatal life. These fetishized objects are therefore by no means mere accessories, nor are they merely cultural signs among others: they symbolize an inward transcendence, that phantasy of a centre-point in reality which nourishes all mytho-logical consciousness, all individual consciousness – that phantasy whereby a projected detail comes to stand for the ego, and the rest of the world is then organized around it. The phantasy of authenticity is sublime, and it is always located somewhere short of reality (*sub limina*). Like the holy relic,[8] whose function it secularizes, the antique object reorganizes the world in a dispersive fashion which is quite antithetical to the extensive nature of functional organization – such organization being the very thing, in fact, from which it seeks to protect the profound and no doubt vital lack of realism of the inner self.

As symbol of the inscription of value in a closed circle and in a perfect time, mythological objects constitute a discourse no longer addressed to others but solely to oneself. Islands of legend, such objects carry human beings back beyond time to their childhood –

8. The significance of the relic is that it makes it possible to enshrine the identity of God or that of the soul of a dead person within an object. And there is no relic without a reliquary: the value 'slides' from the one to the other, and the reliquary, often made of gold, becomes the unmistakable signifier of authenticity, and hence more effective as a symbol.

or perhaps even farther still, back to a pre-birth reality where pure subjectivity was free to conflate itself metaphorically with its surroundings, so that those surroundings became simply the perfect discourse directed by human beings to themselves.

Synchronism, Diachronism, Anachronism

Within the private environment, mythological objects constitute a realm of even greater privacy: they serve less as possessions than as symbolic intercessors – as ancestors, so to speak, than which nothing is more 'private'. They are a way of escaping from everyday life, and no escape is more radical than escape in time, none so thoroughgoing as escape into one's own childhood.[9] Perhaps there is something of this metaphorical escape in all aesthetic feeling, but the work of art as such calls for a rational reading, whereas the antique does not: antiques partake of 'legend', because they are defined first and foremost by their mythical quality, by their coefficient of authenticity. The antique as directly experienced is quite unaffected by period or style, whether the object is a model or whether it is serial in character, whether or not it is precious, or whether it is genuine or fake: it remains in all cases 'perfect'; it is neither internal nor external, but 'elsewhere'; neither synchronic nor diachronic, but *anachronistic*; relative to its possessor, it is neither the complement of a verb 'to be' nor the object of a verb 'to have', but falls, rather, into the grammatical category of an internal object that gives expression to the essence of the verb in an almost tautological manner.

The functional object is devoid of being. Reality prevents its regression to that 'perfect' dimension the fact of proceeding from which suffices to ensure being. This is why such objects seem so reduced, for whatever their price, merit or prestige, they configure, and must perforce continue to configure, the loss of the Father and the Mother. Rich in functionality but impoverished in meaning,

9. Travelling as a tourist always involves going in search of lost time.

their frame of reference is the present moment, and their possibilities do not extend beyond everyday life. The mythological
object, on the other hand, has minimal function and maximal
meaning, while its frame of reference is the ancestral realm –
perhaps even the realm of the absolute anteriority of nature. On
the plane of direct experience, however, the antithetical traits of
the mythological and the functional coexist in complementary
fashion within the one system. Our architect, for example, has
both oil heating and a peasant-style warming-pan. Similarly, a
literary work may be available at the same time in paperback and
in a limited edition or fine binding, an electric washing machine
may cohabit with an old battledore, or a functional built-in
cupboard may be found cheek by jowl with a prominently
displayed Spanish cabinet.[10] This complementarity may even
be discerned in the now common practice of dual residence, of
combining a flat in the city and a house in the country.[11]

   This duel between objects is fundamentally a duel of consciousness; it indicates a failure – and the attempt to redress that failure in a
regressive fashion. In a civilization where synchronism and diachron-
ism strive to establish systematic and exclusive control over reality, a
third dimension, that of anachronism, nevertheless emerges (and this

10. We should not seek one-to-one correspondences here, however, because
the functional field of modern objects is configured in quite a different way
from that of antiques. Moreover, the function of antique objects in this
context exists only in the sense of a function that is extinct.
11. This splitting of the traditional single home into principal and secondary –
or functional and 'naturalized' – residences offers the clearest possible illustration of the systematizing process: the system splits into two in order to strike a
balance between terms that are formally antithetical yet fundamentally
complementary. This split affects the whole of everyday life, as witness an
organization of work and leisure wherein leisure by no means transcends or
even provides an outlet from productive activity: instead, a selfsame everyday
reality splits into two as a means of overriding the contradictions and imposing
itself as a coherent and definitive system. It is true that this process is less
marked in the case of isolated objects; the fact remains that every functional
object is potentially capable of splitting in this way, of *becoming formally opposed
to itself so as to fit more effectively into the overall system.*

as much at the level of objects as at the level of behaviours and social structures). This regressive dimension, though it attests to a relative setback for the system, nevertheless finds a place within that system and even, paradoxically, enables the system to function.

Reverse Projection:
The Technical Object and Primitive Man

Naturally, this ambiguous coexistence of modern functionality and traditional 'décor' arises only after a certain level of economic development, industrial production and practical environmental saturation has been attained. Less privileged social strata (peasants, workers) and 'primitive' peoples have no interest in what is old: they aspire to the functional. All the same, there is a similarity here between 'primitive' and 'civilized' attitudes. When a 'savage' grabs a watch or a fountain pen merely because it is a 'Western' object, we find this behaviour comical or absurd, for the object is not being given its true meaning but appropriated hungrily in accordance with an infantile type of relationship involving a power phantasy. Instead of having a function, the object has a virtue: it has become a sign. Yet is this not the very same procedure of impulsive acculturation and magical appropriation that drives 'civilized' people towards six-teenth-century woodcuts or icons? In both cases what is being acquired under the form of the object is a 'virtue': the 'savage' acquires modern technology, the 'civilized' person acquires ancestral significance. The 'virtue' is not of the same order in the two instances, however. What 'under-developed' people want from the object is an image of the Father as *Power* – in the event, *colonial* power;[12] what

12. In the case of the child, too, objects in the environment come in the first place from the Father (and in early infancy from a phallic mother). To appropriate these objects is to appropriate the power of the Father (as Roland Barthes shows, apropos of motorcars, in 'La voiture, projection de l'ego', *Réaltés*, no. 213, October 1963). The exercise of this power parallels the process of identification with the Father, and embraces all the conflicts this entails; consequently it is always ambiguous and partly aggressive in character.

nostalgic 'civilized' people want is an image of the Father signifying *birth* and value. In the first case, a projective myth; in the second, a retrogressive one. A myth of power – and a myth of origins: whatever it is that man lacks is invested in the object. The 'underdeveloped' fetishize power by means of the technical object; technically advanced, 'civilized' people, for their part, fetishize birth and authenticity by means of the mythological object.

This being said, the fetishism itself is identical. In the last reckoning every antique is beautiful *merely because it has survived, and thus become the sign of an earlier life.* It is our fraught curiosity about our origins that prompts us to place such mythological objects, the signs of a previous order of things, alongside the functional objects which, for their part, are the signs of our current mastery. For we want at one and the same time to be entirely self-made and yet be descended from someone: to succeed the Father yet simultaneously to proceed from the Father. Perhaps mankind will never manage to choose between embarking on the Promethean project of reorganizing the world, thus taking the place of the Father, and being directly descended from an original being. Our objects bear silent witness to this unresolved ambivalence. Some serve as mediation with the present, others as mediation with the past, the value of the latter being that they address a lack. Antiques are preceded by a particle, so to speak, and their inherited nobility compensates for the premature aging of modern objects. There was a time when old people were beautiful because they were 'closer to God' and richer in experience; our technological civilization has rejected the wisdom of the old, but it bows down before the solidity of old things, whose unique value is sealed and certain.

The Market in Antiques

More is involved here than a snobbish and status-seeking itch of the kind evoked by Vance Packard, for example, when he describes how fashionable Bostonians install old panes of a purplish tinge in their windows: 'The defectiveness of those panes is highly cherished even when their functional value is dubious. The panes were part of a shipment of inferior glass foisted off on Americans by English glassmakers more than three centuries ago.'[13] Or again: 'It was found that, if a suburbanite aspires to move up into the "lower-upper class, he will buy antiques – symbols of old social position bought with new money".'[14] Yet social standing may be signalled in a thousand ways (by a car, a modern detached house, etc.), so why is the reference to the *past* so often chosen as a vector of status?[15] All acquired value tends to metamorphose into inherited value, into a received grace. But since blood, birth and titles of nobility have lost their ideological force, the task of signifying transcendence has fallen to material signs – to pieces of furniture, objects, jewellery and works of art of every time and every place. The door has thus been opened to a mass of 'authoritative' signs and idols (whose authenticity, in the end, is neither here nor there); the market has been invaded by a whole magical flora of real or fake furniture, manuscripts and icons. The past in its entirety has been pressed into the service of consumption. This has even created a kind of black market. The New Hebrides, Romanesque Spain and flea markets everywhere have already been stripped clean by the voracious appetite for nostalgia and primitivism of the Western world's bourgeois interiors. Statues of the Virgin and saints are stolen from churches, paintings are stolen from museums, then this booty is sold secretly to rich people whose residences are too new to give them the kind of satisfaction they want. It is a cultural irony – but an economic fact – that this thirst for 'authenticity' can now be slaked only by forgeries.

13. *The Status Seekers* (New York: David McKay, 1959), p. 68.
14. Ibid.
15. Certainly this tendency increases in a general way as people climb the social ladder, but it really takes off only once a certain status and a minimal level of 'urban acculturation' have been reached.

Cultural Neo-Imperialism

Fundamentally, the imperialism that subjugates nature with technical objects and the one that domesticates cultures with antiques are one and the same. This same private imperialism is the organizing principle of a functionally domesticated environment made up of domesticated signs of the past – of ancestral objects, sacred in essence but desacralized, which are called upon to exude their sacredness (or historicalness) into a history-less domesticity.

In this way the entire past, as a repertory of forms of consumption, is incorporated into the repertory of present-day forms in order to constitute a kind of transcendent sphere of fashion.

II A Marginal System: Collecting

Littré's dictionary defines '*objet*' in one of its meanings as 'anything which is the cause or subject of a passion; figuratively – and *par excellence* – the loved object'.

Let us grant that our everyday objects are in fact objects of a passion – the passion for private property, emotional investment in which is every bit as intense as investment in the 'human' passions. Indeed, the everyday passion for private property is often stronger than all the others, and sometimes even reigns supreme, all other passions being absent. It is a measured, diffuse, regulating passion whose fundamental role in the vital equilibrium of the subject or the group – in the very decision to live – we tend not to gauge very well. Apart from the uses to which we put them at any particular moment, objects in this sense have another aspect which is intimately bound up with the subject: no longer simply material bodies offering a certain resistance, they become mental precincts over which I hold sway, they become things of which I am the meaning, they become my property and my passion.

The Object Abstracted from Its Function

If I use a refrigerator to refrigerate, it is a practical mediation: it is not an object but a refrigerator. And in that sense I do not possess it. A *utensil* is never possessed, because a utensil refers one to the world; what is possessed is always an object *abstracted from its function and thus brought into relationship with the subject*. In this context all owned objects partake of the same *abstractness*, and refer to one another only inasmuch as they refer solely to the subject. Such objects together make up the system through which the subject strives to construct a world, a private totality.

Every object thus has two functions – to be put to use and to be possessed. The first involves the field of the world's practical totalization by the subject, the second an abstract totalization of the subject undertaken by the subject himself outside the world. These two functions stand in inverse ratio to each other. At one extreme, the strictly practical object acquires a social status: this is the case with the machine. At the opposite extreme, the pure object, devoid of any function or completely abstracted from its use, takes on a strictly subjective status: it becomes part of a collection. It ceases to be a carpet, a table, a compass or a knick-knack and becomes an object in the sense in which a collector will say 'a beautiful object' rather than specifying it, for example, as 'a beautiful statuette'. An object no longer specified by its function is defined by the subject, but in the passionate abstractness of possession all objects are equivalent. And just one object no longer suffices: the fulfilment of the project of possession always means a succession or even a complete series of objects. This is why owning absolutely any object is always so satisfying and so disappointing at the same time: a whole series lies behind any single object, and makes it into a source of anxiety. Things are not so different on the sexual plane: whereas the love relationship has as its aim a unique being, the need to *possess* the love object can be satisfied only by a succession of objects, by repetition, or, alternatively, by making the assumption that all possible objects are somehow present. Only a more or less complex organization of objects, each of which refers to all the others, can endow each with an abstractness such that the subject will be able to grasp it in that lived abstractness which is the experience of possession.

Collecting is precisely that kind of organization. Our ordinary environment is always ambiguous: functionality is forever collapsing into subjectivity, and possession is continually getting entangled with utility, as part of the ever-disappointed effort to achieve a total integration. Collecting, however, offers a model here: through collecting, the passionate pursuit of possession finds fulfilment and the everyday prose of objects is transformed into poetry, into a triumphant unconscious discourse.

The Object as Passion

'The taste for collection', says Maurice Rheims, 'is a kind of passionate game.'[16] For children, collecting is a rudimentary way of mastering the outside world, of arranging, classifying and manipulating. The most active time for childhood collecting is apparently between the ages of seven and twelve, during the latency period between early childhood and puberty. The urge to collect tends to wane with the onset of puberty, only to re-emerge as soon as that stage has passed. In later life, it is men over forty who most frequently fall victim to this passion. In short, there is in all cases a manifest connection between collecting and sexuality, and this activity appears to provide a powerful compensation during critical stages of sexual development. This tendency clearly runs counter to active genital sexuality, although it is not simply a substitute for it. Rather, as compared with genitality, it constitutes a regression to the anal stage, which is characterized by accumulation, orderliness, aggressive retention, and so on. The activity of collecting is not in any sense equivalent to a sexual practice, for it is not designed to procure instinctual satisfaction (as in fetishism, for example); it may nevertheless produce intense satisfaction as a reaction. The object here takes on the full significance of a loved object: 'Passion for the object leads to its being looked upon as a thing made by God. A collector of porcelain eggs is liable to believe that God never created a form more beautiful or more singular, and indeed that He devised this form solely for the greater delight of collectors.'[17] Collectors are forever

16. *La vie étrange des objets* (Paris: Plon, 1959), p. 28 [*Translator's note*: There is an English translation by David Pryce-Jones: *Art on the Market* (London: Weidenfeld & Nicolson, 1961). I have not used it here.]
17. Ibid., p. 33.

saying that they are 'crazy about' this or that object, and they all without exception – even where the perversion of fetishism plays no part – cloak their collection in an atmosphere of clandestineness and concealment, of secrecy and sequestration, which in every way suggests a feeling of guilt. It is this passionate involvement which lends a touch of the sublime to the regressive activity of collecting; it is also the basis of the view that anyone who does not collect something is 'nothing but a moron, a pathetic human wreck'.[18]

The collector's sublimity, then, derives not from the nature of the objects he collects (which will vary according to his age, profession and social milieu) but from his fanaticism. And this fanaticism is identical whether it characterizes a rich connoisseur of Persian miniatures or a collector of matchboxes. The distinction that may legitimately be drawn here, to the effect that the collector loves his objects on the basis of their membership in a series, whereas the connoisseur loves his on account of their varied and unique charm, is not a decisive one. In both cases gratification flows from the fact that possession depends, on the one hand, on the absolute singularity of each item, a singularity which puts that item on a par with an animate being – indeed, fundamentally on a par with the subject himself – and, on the other hand, on the possibility of a series, and hence of an infinite play of substitutions. Collecting is thus qualitative in its essence and quantitative in its practice. If the feeling of possession is based on a confusion of the senses (of hand and eye) and an intimacy with the privileged object, it is also based just as much on searching, ordering, playing and assembling. In short, there is something of the harem about collecting, for the whole attraction may be summed up as that of an intimate series (one term of which is at any given time the favourite) combined with a serial intimacy.

Man never comes so close to being the master of a secret seraglio as when he is surrounded by his objects. Human relationships,

18. M. Fauron, president of the cigar-band collectors' association, in *Liens* (review of the Club français du Livre), May 1964.

home of uniqueness and conflict, never permit any such fusion of absolute singularity with infinite seriality – which is why they are such a continual source of anxiety. By contrast, the sphere of objects, consisting of successive and homologous terms, reassures. True, such reassurance is founded on an illusion, a trick, a process of abstraction and regression, but no matter. In the words of Maurice Rheims: 'For man, the object is a sort of insentient dog which accepts his blandishments and returns them after its own fashion, or rather which returns them like a mirror faithful not to real images but to images that are desired.'[19]

The Finest of Domestic Animals

Rheims's dog image is the right one, for pets are indeed an intermediate category between human beings and objects. The pathos-laden presence of a dog, a cat, a tortoise or a canary is a testimonial to a failure of the interhuman relationship and an attendant recourse to a narcissistic domestic universe where subjectivity finds fulfilment in the most quietistic way. Note, by the way, that these animals are not sexed (indeed, they are often neutered for their role as household pets); they are every bit as devoid of sex, even though they are alive, as objects are. This is the price to be paid if they are to provide emotional security: only their actual or symbolic castration makes it possible for them to serve as mitigators of their owners' castration anxiety. This is a part that all the objects that surround us also play to perfection. The object is in fact the finest of domestic animals – the only 'being' whose qualities exalt rather than limit my person. In the plural, objects are the only entities in existence that can genuinely coexist, because the differences between them do not set them against one another, as happens in the case of living beings: instead they all converge submissively upon me and accumulate with the greatest of ease in my consciousness. Nothing can be both 'personalized'

19. Rheims, *La vie étrange des objets*, p. 50.

and quantified so easily as objects. Moreover, this subjective quantifiability is not restricted: everything can be possessed, cathected or (in the activity of collecting) organized, classified and assigned a place. The object is thus in the strict sense of the word a mirror, for the images it reflects can only follow upon one another without ever contradicting one another. And indeed, as a mirror the object is perfect, precisely because it sends back not real images, but desired ones. In a word, it is a dog of which nothing remains but faithfulness. What is more, you can look at an object without it looking back at you. *That is why everything that cannot be invested in human relationships is invested in objects.* That is why regression of this kind is so easy, why people so readily practise this form of 'retreat'. But we must not allow ourselves to be taken in by this, nor by the vast literature that sentimentalizes inanimate objects. The 'retreat' involved here really is a regression, and the passion mobilized is a passion for flight. Objects undoubtedly serve in a regulatory capacity with regard to everyday life, dissipating many neuroses and providing an outlet for all kinds of tensions and for energies that are in mourning. This is what gives them their 'soul', what makes them 'ours' – but it is also what turns them into the décor of a tenacious mythology, the ideal décor for an equilibrium that is itself neurotic.

A Serial Game

Yet this mediation would seem to be a poor one. How can consciousness let itself be fooled in this way? Such is the cunning of subjectivity: an object that is possessed can never be a poor mediation. It is always absolutely singular. Not in reality, of course: the possession of a 'rare' or 'unique' object is obviously the ideal aim of its appropriation, but for one thing the proof that a given object is unique can never be supplied in a real world, and, for another, consciousness gets along just fine without proof. The particular value of the object, its exchange value, is a function of cultural and social determinants. Its absolute singularity, on the other hand, arises from the fact of being possessed by me – and this allows me, in turn, to recognize myself in the object as an absolutely singular being. This is a grandiose tautology, but one that gives the relationship to objects all its density – its absurd facility, and the illusory but intense gratification it supplies.[20] What is more, while this closed circuit may also govern human relationships (albeit less easily), the relationship with objects has one characteristic that can never be found in the intersubjective realm: no object ever opposes the extension of the process of narcissistic projection to an unlimited number of other objects; on the contrary, the object imposes that very tendency, thereby contributing to the creation of a total environment, to that totalization of images of the self that is the basis of the miracle of collecting. For what you really collect is always yourself.

This makes it easier to understand the structure of the system of possession: any collection comprises a succession of items, but the last in the set is the person of the collector. Reciprocally, the person of the collector is constituted as such only if it replaces each item in the collection in turn. An analogous structure on the sociological level is to be found in the system of model and series: both the series and the collection serve to institute possession of the object – that is, they facilitate the mutual integration of object and person.[21]

20. It also creates disillusion, of course, itself bound up with the tautological character of the system.

21. The *series* is practically always a kind of game that makes it possible to select any one term and invest it with the privileged status of a *model*. A child is throwing bottle-tops: which one will go the farthest? It is no coincidence if the same one always comes out ahead: this is his favourite. The model he thus constructs, the hierarchy he sets up, is in fact himself – for he does not identify himself with one bottle-top but, rather, with the fact that one bottle-top always wins. And he is just as present in each of the other tops, unmarked terms in the antagonism between winner and losers: throwing the bottle-tops one by one is playing at constituting oneself as a series in order then to constitute oneself as a model. Here, in a nutshell, is the psychology of the collector; and a collector who collects only privileged or 'unique' objects is simply making sure that he himself is the object that always wins.

From Quantity to Quality: The Unique Object

It may well be objected here that any exclusive passion for a single object on the part of an art lover suffices to demolish our hypothesis. It is quite clear, however, that the unique object is in fact simply the final term, the one which sums up all the others, that it is the supreme component of an entire paradigm (albeit a virtual, invisible or implicit one) – that it is, in short, the emblem of the series.

In the portraits in which he illustrates the passion of curiosity, La Bruyère puts the following words into the mouth of a collector of fine prints: 'I suffer from a grave affliction which will surely oblige me to abandon all thought of prints till the end of my days: I have all of Callot except for one – and one which, to be frank, is not among his best works. Indeed, it is one of his worst, yet it would round out Callot for me. I have searched high and low for this print for twenty years, and I now despair of ever finding it.' The equivalence experienced here between the whole series minus one and the final term missing from the series is conveyed with arithmetical certainty.[22] The absent final term is a symbolic distillation of that series without which it would not exist; consequently it acquires a strange quality, a quality which is the quintessence of the whole quantitative calibration of the series. This term is the unique object, defined by its final position and hence creating the illusion that it embodies a particular goal or end. This is all well and good, but it shows us how it is quantity that impels towards quality, and how the value thus concentrated on this simple signifier is in fact indistinguishable from the value that infuses the whole chain of intermediate signifiers of the paradigm. This is what might be called the symbolism of the object, in the etymological sense (cf. Greek *sumballein*, to put together), in accordance with which a chain of signifiers may be

22. Any term in the series may become the final term: any Callot can be the one to 'round out Callot'.

summed up in just one of its terms. The object is the symbol not of some external agency or value but first and foremost of the whole series of objects of which it is the (final) term. (This in addition to symbolizing the person whose object it is.)

La Bruyère's example illustrates another rule, too: that the object attains exceptional value only by virtue of its absence. This is not simply a matter of covetousness. *One cannot but wonder whether collections are in fact meant to be completed,* whether lack does not play an essential part here – a positive one, moreover, as the means whereby the subject reapprehends his own objectivity. If so, the *presence* of the final object of the collection would basically signify the death of the subject, whereas its absence would be what enables him merely to rehearse his death (and so exorcize it) by having an object represent it. This lack is experienced as suffering, but it is also the breach that makes it possible to avoid completing the collection and thus definitively erasing reality. Let us therefore applaud La Bruyère's collector for never finding his last Callot, for if he had done so he would thereby have ceased to be the living and passionate man that he still was, after all. It might be added that madness begins once a collection is deemed complete and thus ceases to centre around its absent term.

This account of things is buttressed by another story told by Maurice Rheims. A bibliophile specializing in unique copies learns one day that a New York bookseller is offering a book that is identical to one of his prize possessions. He rushes to New York, acquires the book, summons a lawyer, has the offending second copy burnt before him and elicits an affidavit substantiating this act of destruction. Once he is back home, he inserts this legal document in his copy, now once again unique, and goes to bed happy. Should we conclude that in this case the *series* has been abolished? Not at all. It only seems so, because the collector's original copy was in fact invested with the value of all virtual copies, and by destroying the rival copy the book collector was merely reinstituting the perfection of a compromised symbol. Whether denied, forgotten, destroyed, or merely virtual, the series is still present. The serial nature of the most mundane of everyday objects, as of the most transcendent of rarities, is what nourishes the relationship of ownership and the possibility of passionate play: without seriality no such play would be conceivable, hence no possession – and hence, too, properly speaking, no object. A truly unique, absolute object, an object such that it has no antecedents and is in no way dispersed in some series or other – such an object is unthinkable. It has no more existence than a pure sound. Just as harmonic series bring sounds up to their perceived quality, so paradigmatic series, whatever their degree of complexity, bring objects up to their symbolic quality – carrying them, in the same movement, into the sphere of the human relationship of mastery and play.

Objects and Habits: Wrist-Watches

Every object oscillates between a practical specificity, a function which is in a sense its manifest discourse, and absorption by a series or collection where it becomes one term in a latent, repetitive discourse – the most basic and tenacious of discourses. This discursive system of objects is analogous to the system of habits.[23]

Habits imply discontinuity and repetition – not continuity, as common usage suggests. By breaking up time, our 'habitual' patterns dispel the anxiety-provoking aspect of the temporal continuum and of the absolute singularity of events. Similarly, it is thanks to their discontinuous integration into series that we put objects at our sole disposition, that we own them. This is the discourse of subjectivity itself, and objects are a privileged register of that discourse. Between the world's irreversible evolution and ourselves, objects interpose a discontinuous, classifiable, reversible

23. Moreover, any object immediately becomes the foundation of a network of habits, the focus of a set of behavioural routines. Conversely, there is probably no habit that does not centre on an object. In everyday existence the two are inextricably bound up with each other.

screen which can be reconstituted at will, a segment of the world which belongs to us, responding to our hands and minds and delivering us from anxiety. Objects do not merely help us to master the world by virtue of their integration into instrumental series, they also help us, *by virtue of their integration into mental series*, to master time, rendering it discontinuous and classifying it, after the fashion of habits, and subjecting it to the same associational constraints as those which govern the arrangement of things in space.

There is no better illustration of this discontinuous and 'habitual' function than the wrist-watch.[24] The watch epitomizes the duality of the way we experience objects. On the one hand, it tells us the actual time; and chronometric precision is *par excellence* the dimension of practical constraints, of society as external to us, and of death. As well as subjecting us to an irreducible temporality, however, the watch as an object helps us to appropriate time: just as the automobile 'eats up' miles, so the watch-object eats up time.[25] By making time into a substance that can be divided up, it turns it into an object to be consumed. A perilous dimension of praxis is thus transformed into a domesticated quantity. Beyond just knowing the time, 'possessing' the time in and through an object that is one's own, having the time continuously recorded before one's eyes, has become a crutch, a necessary reassurance, for civilized man. The time is no longer in the home, no longer the clock's beating heart, but its registration on the wrist continues to ensure the same organic satisfaction as the regular throbbing of an internal organ. Thanks to my watch, time presents itself simulta-

24. The watch is also indicative (as is the disappearance of clocks) of the irresistible tendency of modern objects towards miniaturization and individualization. It is also the oldest, the smallest, the closest to us, and the most valuable of personal machines – an intimate and highly cathected mechanical talisman which becomes the object of everyday complicity, fascination (especially for children), and jealousy.
25. Exactness about time parallels speed in space: time has to be gobbled up as completely as possible.

neously as the very dimension of my objectification and as a simple household necessity. As a matter of fact, any object might be used to demonstrate how even the dimension of objective constraint is incorporated by everyday experience; the watch, however, is the best example, by virtue of its explicit relationship to time.

Objects and Time: A Controlled Cycle

The problem of time is a fundamental aspect of collecting. As Maurice Rheims says: 'A phenomenon that often goes hand in hand with the passion for collecting is the loss of any sense of the present time.'[26] But is this really just a matter of an escape into nostalgia? Certainly, someone who identifies with Louis XVI down to the feet of his armchairs, or develops a true passion for sixteenth-century snuffboxes, is marking himself off from the present by means of a historical reference, yet this reference takes second place to his direct experience of collecting's systematic aspect. The deep-rooted power of collected objects stems neither from their uniqueness nor from their historical distinctiveness. It is not because of such considerations that the temporality of collecting is not real time but, rather, *because the organization of the collection itself replaces time.* And no doubt this is the collection's fundamental function: the resolving of real time into a systematic dimension. Taste, particularity, status, the discourse of society – any of these may cause the collection to open onto a broader relationship (though this will never go beyond a group of insiders); in all cases, however, the collection must remain, literally, a 'pastime'. Indeed, it abolishes time. More precisely, by reducing time to a fixed set of terms navigable in either direction, the collection represents the continual recommencement of a controlled cycle whereby man, at any moment and with complete confidence, starting with any term and sure of returning to it, is able to set his game of life and death in motion.

26. *La vie étrange des objets*, p. 42.

A Marginal System: Collecting

It is in this sense that the environment of private objects and their possession (collection being the most extreme instance) is a dimension of our life which, though imaginary, is absolutely essential. Just as essential as dreams. It has been said that if dreams could be experimentally suppressed, serious mental disturbances would quickly ensue. It is certainly true that were it possible to deprive people of the regressive escape offered by the game of possession, if they were prevented from giving voice to their controlled, self-addressed discourse, from using objects to recite themselves, as it were, outside time, then mental disorder would surely follow immediately, just as in the case of dream deprivation. We cannot live in absolute singularity, in the irreversibility signalled by the moment of birth, and it is precisely this irreversible movement from birth towards death that objects help us to cope with.

Of course the balance thus achieved is a neurotic one; of course this bulwark against anxiety is regressive, for time is objectively irreversible, after all, and even the objects whose function it is to protect us from it are perforce themselves carried off by it; and of course the defence mechanism that imposes discontinuity by means of objects is forever being contested, for the world and human beings are in reality *continuous*. But can we really speak here in terms of normality or anomaly? Taking refuge in a closed synchronicity may certainly be deemed denial of reality and flight if one considers that the object is the recipient of a cathexis that 'ought' to have been invested in human relationships. But this is the price we pay for the vast regulating power of these mechanisms, which today, with the disappearance of the old religious and ideological authorities, are becoming the consolation of consolations, the everyday mythology absorbing all the *angst* that attends time, that attends death.

It should be clear that we are not here promoting any spontaneous mythology according to which man somehow extends his life or survives his death by means of the objects he possesses. The refuge-seeking procedure I have been describing depends not on an immortality, an eternity or a survival founded on the object *qua* reflection (something which man has basically never believed in) but, rather, on a more complex action which 'recycles' birth and death into *a system of objects*. What man gets from objects is not a guarantee of life after death but *the possibility, from the present moment onwards, of continually experiencing the unfolding of his existence in a controlled, cyclical mode, symbolically transcending a real existence the irreversibility of whose progression he is powerless to affect.*

We are not far from the ball which the child (in Freud's account) causes to disappear and reappear in order to experience the absence and presence of its mother alternately (*Fort! Da! Fort! Da!*) – in order to counter her anxiety-provoking absence with this infinite cycle of disappearance and reappearance of the object. The symbolic implications of play within the series are not hard to discern here, and we may sum them up by saying that the object is *the thing with which we construct our mourning*: the object represents our own death, but that death is transcended (symbolically) by virtue of the fact that we *possess* the object; the fact that by introjecting it into a work of mourning – by integrating it into a series in which its absence and its re-emergence elsewhere 'work' at replaying themselves continually, recurrently – we succeed in dispelling the anxiety associated with absence and with the reality of death. Objects allow us to apply the work of mourning to ourselves right now, in everyday life, and this in turn allows us to live – to live regressively, no doubt, but at least to live. A person who collects is dead, but he literally survives himself through his collection, which (even while he lives) duplicates him infinitely, beyond death, *by integrating death itself into the series, into the cycle.* Once again the parallel with dreams applies here. If any object's function – practical, cultural or social – means that it is the mediation of a *wish*, it is also, as one term among others in the systematic game that we have been describing, the voice of *desire*. Desire is, in fact, the motor of the repetition or substitution of oneself, along the infinite chain of signifiers, through or beyond death. And if the function of dreams is to ensure the continuity of sleep, that of objects, thanks to very much the same sort of compromise, is to ensure the continuity of life.[27]

The Sequestered Object: Jealousy

At the terminal point of its regressive movement, the passion for objects ends up as pure jealousy. The joy of possession in its most profound form now derives from the value that objects can have for others and from the fact of depriving them thereof. This jealous complex, though it is characteristic of the collector at his most fanatical, presides also, proportionately speaking, over the simplest proprietary reflex. A powerful anal-sadistic impulse, it produces the urge to sequester beauty so as to be the only one to enjoy it: a kind of sexually perverse behaviour widely present in a diffuse form in the relationship to objects.

What does the sequestered object represent? (Its objective value is secondary, of course – its attraction lies in the very fact of its confinement.) If you do not lend your car, your fountain pen or your wife to anyone, that is because these objects, according to the logic of jealousy, are narcissistic equivalents of the ego: to lose

27. A story told by Tristan Bernard provides an amusing illustration of the fact that collecting is a way of playing with death (that is, a passion), and in consequence stronger, symbolically, than death itself. There was once a man who collected children: legitimate, illegitimate, children of a first or a second marriage, foundlings, by-blows, and so on. One day he gave a house party at which his entire 'collection' were present: a cynical friend of his remarked, however, 'There is one kind of child you do not have.' 'What type?' the host wanted to know. 'A posthumous child,' came the answer. Whereupon this passionate collector first got his wife pregnant and promptly thereafter committed suicide.

The same system is to be found, minus the narrative trappings, in games of chance. This is the reason for their fascination, which is even more intense than that of collecting. Such games imply a pure transcendence of death: subjectivity cathects the pure series with an imaginary mastery, quite certain that whatever the ups and downs of the play, no one has the power to reintroduce into it the *real* conditions of life and death.

them, or for them to be damaged, means castration. The phallus, to put it in a nutshell, is not something one loans out. What the jealous owner sequesters and cleaves to is his own libido, in the shape of an object, which he is striving to exorcize by means of a system of confinement – the same system, in fact, by virtue of which collecting dispels anxiety about death. He castrates himself out of anguish about his own sexuality; or, more exactly, he uses a symbolic castration – sequestration – pre-emptively, as a way of countering anxiety about *real* castration.[28] This desperate strategy is the basis of the horrible gratification that jealousy affords. For one is always jealous of oneself. It is oneself that one locks up and guards so closely. And it is from oneself that one obtains gratification.

Obviously, this jealous pleasure occurs in a context of absolute disillusionment, because systematic regression can never completely eradicate consciousness of the real world or of the futility of such behaviour. The same goes for collecting, whose sway is fragile at best, for the sway of the real world lies ever just behind it, and is continually threatening it. Yet this disillusionment is itself part of the system – indeed, is as responsible as satisfaction for setting the system in motion: disillusionment never refers to the world but, rather, to an ulterior term; disillusionment and satisfaction occupy sequential positions in the cycle. The neurotic activation of the system is thus attributable to this constitutive disillusionment. In such cases the series tends to run its course at a faster and faster pace, chasing its tail as differences wear out and the substitution mechanism speeds up. The system may even enter a destructive phase, implying the self-destruction of the subject. Maurice Rheims evokes the ritualized 'execution' of collections – a kind of suicide based on the impossibility of ever circumscribing death. It is not rare in the context of the system of jealousy for the subject eventually to destroy the sequestered object or being out of a

28. Of course this also goes for pets, and by extension for the 'object' in the sexual relationship, whose manipulation in jealousy is of a similar kind.

feeling that he can never completely rid himself of the adversity of the world, and of his own sexuality. This is the logical and illogical end of his passion.[29]

The Object Destructured: Perversion

The effectiveness of the system of possession is directly linked to its regressive character. And this regression in turn is linked to the very *modus operandi* of perversion. If perversion as it concerns objects is most clearly discernible in the crystallized form of fetishism, we are perfectly justified in noting how throughout the system, organized according to the same aims and functioning in the same ways, the possession of objects and the passion for them is, shall we say, *a tempered mode of sexual perversion*. Indeed, just as possession depends on the discontinuity of the series (real or virtual) and on the choice of a privileged term within it, so sexual perversion is founded on the inability to apprehend the other *qua* object of desire in his or her unique totality as a person, to grasp the other in any but a discontinuous way: the other is transformed into the paradigm of various eroticized parts of the body, a single one of which becomes the focus of objectification. A particular woman is no longer a woman but merely a sex, breasts, belly, thighs, voice and face – and preferably just one of them.[30] She thus becomes a constituent 'object' in a series whose different terms are gazetted by desire, and whose real referent is by no means the

29. We must not confuse disillusionment, an internal motor of the regressive system of the series, with the lack we spoke of above, which on the contrary tends to foster emergence from the system. Disillusionment causes the subject to tighten his retrogressive embrace of the series; lack causes him to evolve (relatively speaking) in the direction of the outside world.
30. The regressive tendency, ever more specialized and impersonal, may converge on the hair or the feet, or, ultimately, crystallize – at the opposite pole to any living being – on a garter or a brassiere; we thus come back to the material object, whose possession may be described as the perfect way of eliminating the presence of the other.

loved person but, rather, the subject himself, collecting and eroticizing himself and turning the relationship of love into a discourse directed towards him alone.

The opening sequence in Jean-Luc Godard's film *Contempt* clearly illustrates this. The dialogue in this 'nude' scene goes as follows.

'Do you love my feet?' the woman asks. (Note that throughout the scene she is inventorying herself in a mirror – this is not irrelevant, because in this way she attributes value to herself *as she is seen*, via her image, and thus, already, as spatially discontinuous.)

'Yes, I love them.'

'Do you love my legs?'

'Yes.'

'And my thighs?'

'Yes,' he replies once more. 'I love them.'

(And so on, from foot to head, ending up with her hair.)

'So, you love me totally?'

'Yes, I love you totally.'

'Me too, Paul,' she says, summing up the situation.

It may be that the film's makers saw all this as the clarifying algebra of a demystified love. Be that as it may, such a grotesque reconstruction of desire is the height of inhumanity. Once broken down by body parts into a series, the woman as pure object is then reintegrated into the greater series of all woman-objects, where she is merely one term among others. The only activity possible within the logic of this system is the play of substitutions. This was what we recognized earlier as the motor of satisfaction in the collector.

In the love relationship the tendency to break the object down into discrete details in accordance with a perverse autoerotic system is slowed by the living unity of the other person.[31] When it comes to material objects, however, and especially to manu-

31. This explains why the passionate feelings are transferred to the fetish, whose function is a radical simplification of the living sexual object which makes this object equivalent to the penis and cathects it accordingly.

factured objects complex enough to lend themselves to mental dismantling, this tendency has free rein. With the automobile, for instance, it is possible to speak of '*my* brakes', '*my* tail fins', '*my* steering wheel'; or to say '*I* am braking', '*I* am turning' or '*I* am starting'. In short, all the car's 'organs' and functions may be brought separately into relation with the person of the owner in the possessive mode. We are dealing here not with a process of personalization at the social level but with a process of a projective kind. We are concerned not with *having* but with *being*. With the horse, despite the fact that this animal was a remarkable instrument of power and transcendence for man, this kind of confusion was never possible. The fact is that the horse is not made of pieces – and above all, that it is *sexed*. We can say 'my horse' or 'my wife', but that is as far as this kind of possessive denomination can go. That which has a sex resists fragmenting projection and hence also the mode of appropriation that we have identified as a perversion.[32] Faced by a living being, we may say 'my' but we cannot say 'I' as we do when we symbolically appropriate the functions and 'organs' of a car. That type of regression is not available to us. The horse may be the recipient of powerful symbolic cathexes: we associate it with the wild sexuality of the rutting season, as with the wisdom of the centaur; its head is a terrifying phantasy linked to the image of the father, yet its calm embodies the protective strength of Cheiron the teacher. It is never cathected, however, in the simplistic, narcissistic, far more impoverished and infantile manner in which the ego is projected onto structural details of cars (in accordance with an almost delusional analogy with disassociated parts and functions of the human body). The existence of a dynamic symbolism of the horse may be attributed precisely to the fact that isolated identifications with distinct functions or organs

32. By the same token possessive identification operates in the case of living beings only to the extent that such beings may be perceived as asexual: 'Does our head hurt?', we may say to a baby. When we are confronted by a sexed being, however, this kind of confusional identification is halted by castration anxiety.

of the horse are an impossibility; nor is there any prospect, therefore, of collapsing this relationship into an autoerotic 'discourse' concerned with disconnected elements.

Fragmentation and regression of that kind presuppose a technique, but one which has become autonomous at the level of the part-object. A woman broken down into a syntagma of erogenous zones is classified exclusively by the functionality of pleasure, to which the response is an objectivizing and ritualizing erotic technique that masks the anxiety associated with the interpersonal relationship while at the same time serving as a genuine (gestural and effective) dose of reality at the very heart of perversion as a phantasy system. The fact is that every mental system needs a credibility factor of this sort – a foothold in the real, a technical rationale or justification. Thus the accelerator referred to in the words 'I am accelerating', or the whole car implied when we say 'my car', serves as the real, technical justification for a whole realm of narcissistic annexation *short of* reality. The same goes for erotic technique, when it is accepted for what it is; for at this level we are no longer in the genital sphere, which opens onto reality, onto pleasure, but, rather, in a regressive, anal sphere of sexual systematizing for which erotic gestures are merely the justification.

Clearly, then, 'technical' is a very long way indeed from implying 'objective'. Technique does have this quality when it is socialized, when it is adopted by technology, and when it informs new structures. In the everyday realm, however, it constitutes a field that is always hospitable to regressive phantasies, because the possibility of a destructuring is ever imminent. Once assembled and mounted, the components of a technical object imply a certain coherence. But such a structure is always vulnerable to the human mind: held together from without by its function, it is purely formal for the psyche. The hierarchy of its elements can be dismantled at any time, and those elements made interchangeable within a paradigmatic system which the subject uses for his self-recitation. The object is discontinuous already – and certainly easy for thought to disassemble. Moreover, the task is all the easier now that the object – especially the technical object – is no longer lent unity by a set of human gestures and by human energy. Another reason why the car, in contrast to the horse, is such a perfect object for the purposes of narcissistic manipulation is that mastery over the horse is muscular and active, and calls for a gestural system designed to maintain balance, whereas mastery over a car is simplified, functional and abstract.

From Serial Motivation to Real Motivation

Hitherto our discussion has paid no heed whatsoever to the actual nature of the objects that are collected: we have concentrated on the systematic aspects of collecting and ignored the thematic. It is obvious, however, that collecting masterpieces is not exactly the same thing as collecting cigar bands. First of all, a distinction must be drawn between the concept of collection (Latin *colligere*, to choose and gather together) and the concept of accumulation. At the simplest level, matter of one kind or another is accumulated: old papers are piled up, or quantities of food are stored. This activity falls somewhere between oral introjection and anal retention. At a somewhat higher level lies the serial accumulation of identical objects. As for collecting proper, it has a door open onto culture, being concerned with differentiated objects which often have exchange value, which may also be 'objects' of preservation, trade, social ritual, exhibition – perhaps even generators of profit. Such objects are accompanied by projects. And though they remain interrelated, their interplay involves the social world outside, and embraces human relationships.

However powerful external motivations may be, collections can never escape from their internal systematization; at best they may represent a compromise between internal and external factors, and even when a collection transforms itself into a discourse addressed to others, it continues to be first and foremost a discourse addressed to oneself. Serial motivation is discernible everywhere.

Research shows that buyers of books published in series (such as *10/18* or *Que sais-je?*[33]), once they are caught up in collecting, will even acquire titles of no interest to them: the distinctiveness of the book relative to the series itself thus suffices to create a purely formal interest which replaces any real one. The motive of purchase is nothing but this contingent association. A comparable kind of behaviour is that of people who cannot read comfortably unless they are surrounded by all their books; in such cases the specificity of what is being read tends to evaporate. Even farther down the same path, the book itself may count less than the moment when it is put back in its proper place on the shelf. Conversely, once a collector's enthusiasm for a series wanes it is very difficult to revive, and now he may not even buy volumes of genuine interest to him. This is as much evidence as we need to draw a clear distinction between serial motivation and real motivation. The two are mutually exclusive and can coexist only on the basis of compromise, with a notable tendency, founded on inertia, for serial motivation to carry the day over the dialectical motivation of interest.[34]

Mere collecting, however, may sometimes create real interest. The person who sets out to buy every title in the *Que sais-je?* series may end up confining his collection to a single subject, such as music or sociology. Once a certain quantitative threshold is

33. [*Translator's note*: These are well-known series of pocket books in uniform format. *Que sais-je?* is a series of short monographs on a vast array of topics.]
34. This distinction between serial satisfaction and pleasure proper is an essential one. True pleasure is a sort of pleasure-in-pleasure whereby mere satisfaction is transcended as such, and grounds itself in a relationship. In serial satisfaction, by contrast, this second-level pleasure, this qualitative dimension of pleasure, disappears, is missing or unfulfilled. Satisfaction must depend on linear succession alone: an unattainable totality is extended by means of projection and compensated for by means of repetition. People stop reading the books they buy, then proceed to buy more and more. Similarly the repetition of the sexual act, or a multiplicity of sexual partners, may serve indefinitely as an ersatz from of love as exploration. Pleasure in pleasure is gone, only satisfaction remains – and the two are mutually exclusive.

reached, sheer accumulation may occasionally give way to a measure of discrimination. There is no hard-and-fast rule here. Artistic masterpieces *may* be collected with the same regressive fanaticism as cheese labels; on the other hand, children who collect stamps are continually swapping them with their friends. No iron-clad connection exists, therefore, between a collection's thematic complexity and its real openness to the outside world. At best such complexity may give us a clue, may be grounds for a presumption of openness.

A collection can emancipate itself from unalloyed accumulation not only by virtue of its cultural complexity but also by virtue of what is missing from it, by virtue of its incompleteness. A lack here is always a specific demand, an appeal for such and such an absent object. And this demand, in the shape of research, passion, or messages to other people,[35] suffices to shatter that fatal enchantment of the collector which plunges him into a state of pure fascination. A recent television programme on collecting made the point well: every collector who presented his collection to the viewing audience would mention the very special 'object' that he did not have, and invite everyone to find it for him. So, even though objects may on occasion lead into the realm of social discourse, it must be acknowledged that *it is usually not an object's presence but far more often its absence that clears the way for social intercourse.*

A Discourse Addressed to Oneself

It remains characteristic of the collection that sooner or later a radical change will occur capable of wrenching it out of its regressive system and orientating it towards a project or task (whether status-related, cultural or commercial is of no conse-

35. Even in this case, however, the collector tends to call upon other people solely as observers of his collection, integrating them as third parties only in an already constituted subject–object relationship.

quence, just so long as an object eventually brings one human being face to face with another – at which point the object has become a message). All the same, no matter how open a collection is, it will always harbour an irreducible element of non-relationship to the world. Because he feels alienated and abolished by a social discourse whose rules escape him, the collector strives to reconstitute a discourse that is transparent to him, a discourse whose signifiers he controls and whose referent *par excellence* is himself. In this he is doomed to failure: he cannot see that he is simply transforming an open-ended objective discontinuity into a closed subjective one, where even the language he uses has lost any general validity. This kind of totalization by means of objects always bears the stamp of solitude. It fails to communicate with the outside, and communication is missing within it. In point of fact, moreover, we cannot avoid the question whether objects can indeed ever come to constitute any other language than this: can man ever use objects to set up a language that is more than a discourse addressed to himself?

The collector is never an utterly hopeless fanatic, precisely because he collects objects that in some way always prevent him from regressing into the ultimate abstraction of a delusional state, but at the same time the discourse he thus creates can never – for the very same reason – get beyond a certain poverty and infantilism. Collecting is always a limited, repetitive process, and the very material objects with which it is concerned are too concrete and too discontinuous ever to be articulated as a true dialectical structure.[36] So if non-collectors are indeed 'nothing but morons', collectors, for their part, invariably have something impoverished and inhuman about them.

36. As distinct from science or memory, for example – which also involve collecting, but the collecting of facts or knowledge.

C. The Metafunctional and Dysfunctional System: Gadgets and Robots

We have now considered objects from the point of view of their objective systematization (interior design and atmosphere) and from that of their subjective systematization (collecting). Let us next turn our attention to their connotations – and hence to their ideological significance.

Technical Connotation: Automatism

If formal connotation is summed up in the word FASHION,[1] technical connotation is epitomized by the notion of AUTOMATISM, which is the major concept of the modern object's mechanistic triumphalism, the ideal of its mythology. What automatism means is that the object, in its particular function, takes on the connotation of an absolute.[2]

An example borrowed from Gilbert Simondon well illustrates this slipping to technical connotation via the idea of automatism.[3] From the strictly technological standpoint, the elimination of the starting-handle makes the mechanical operation of cars more complicated, because it subordinates it to the use of electrical power from a storage battery that is external to the system. This increased complication – and abstractness – is nevertheless pre-

1. See my account of the rhetoric of forms as 'atmospheric values', above, pp. 47 ff; for the sociological aspects, see 'Models and Series' below.
2. Thus, in the realm of forms, the tail fins of a car connote speed in the absolute, and this on the basis of formal criteria.
3. *Du mode d'existence des objects techniques* (Paris: Aubier, 1958), p. 26.

sented as progress, as a sign of modernity. Thanks to the connotation of automatism, which in fact masks a structural weakness, cars with starting-handles now seem outdated, and those without, modern. Of course, one might argue that the lack of a starting-handle serves a function every bit as real as the handle itself, namely the satisfaction of the desire for automatism. In the same way the chrome-plating and giant tail fins that weigh a car down could be said to serve the function of satisfying the demand for status. But the fulfilment of such secondary functions clearly militates against the material structure of the technical object. Even though so many unintegrated features remain both in the engine and in the external design of cars, the manufacturers tout excessive automatism in accessories as the last word in mechanical achievement. The same goes for the systematic resort to servomechanisms, whose most immediate effect is to render an object more fragile, thus raising its cost, shortening its effective life, and hastening its replacement.

'Functional' Transcendence

The degree to which a machine approaches perfection is thus everywhere presented as proportional to its degree of automatism. The fact is, however, that automating machines means sacrificing a very great deal of potential functionality. In order to automate a practical object, it is necessary to *stereotype it in its function*, thus making it more fragile. Far from having any intrinsic technical advantages, automatism always embodies the risk of arresting technical advance, for so long as an object has not been automated it remains susceptible of redesign, of self-transcendence through incorporation into a larger functional whole. When it becomes automatic, on the other hand, its function is fulfilled, certainly, but it is also hermetically sealed. Automatism amounts to a closing-off, to a sort of functional self-sufficiency which exiles man to the irresponsibility of a mere spectator. Contained within it is the dream of a dominated world, of a formally perfected technicity that serves an inert and dreamy humanity.

Current technological thinking rejects this tendency in principle, and holds that true perfection in machines – one genuinely founded on an increasing level of technicity, and hence expressing true 'functionality' – depends not on more automatism but on a certain margin of indeterminacy which lets the machine respond to information from outside. The highly technical machine is thus an open structure, and a universe of such open-ended machines presupposes man as organizer and living interpreter. But even if the automatizing tendency is repulsed at the highest technological level, the fact remains that in practice it is continually pushing objects into a dangerous abstractness. Automatism is king, and its fascination is indeed so powerful precisely because it is not that of a technical rationality: rather, we come under its spell because we experience it as a basic desire, as *the imaginary truth of the object*, in comparison with which the object's structure and concrete function leave us cold. Consider merely our continual wishing for 'everything to work by itself', for every object to perform this miracle of minimum effort in the carrying out of its assigned function. For the user, automatism means a wondrous absence of activity, and the enjoyment this procures is comparable to that derived, on another plane, from seeing without being seen: an esoteric satisfaction experienced at the most everyday level. The fact that every automated object may lead us into often unchangeable stereotypical behaviour constitutes no real challenge to this immediate demand of ours: the desire for automatism is there first – it takes priority over objective practice. And if it is so firmly rooted that the myth of its formal realization presents an almost material obstacle to the open-ended structuring of techniques and needs, the reason is that it is rooted in objects *as our own image.*[4]

4. Of course there is resistance here and there: a kind of 'heroic' personalization of driving, for instance, causes some people to disdain automatic gear-changing. But like it or not, such 'personal' heroism is destined to disappear.

Because the automated object 'works by itself', its resemblance to the autonomous human being is unmistakable, and the fascination thus created carries the day. We are in the presence of a new anthropomorphism. Formerly the image of man was clearly imprinted in the morphology and the manner of use of tools, of furniture, or of the house itself.[5] In the perfected technical object this compliance has been destroyed, but it has been replaced by a symbolism of superstructural rather than primary functions: it is no longer his gestures, his energy, his needs and the image of his body that man projects into automated objects, but instead the autonomy of his consciousness, his power of control, his own individual nature, his personhood.

This supra-functionality of human consciousness is, in the end, what automatism strives to echo in the object. In a way that parallels the formal self-transcendence of the human individual, automatism aspires to be a sort of *ne plus ultra* of the object, enabling it to transcend its function. And automatism, too, uses a kind of formal abstraction to conceal structural defects, defence mechanisms and objective determinants. That perfect and perfectly autonomous monad which is the governing dream of subjectivity is thus also very clearly the dream that haunts objects. Emancipated from its former naïve animism and too-human meanings, the object finds the elements of its modern mythology in its own technical existence (thanks to the projection into the technical domain of the absolute formal autonomy of individual consciousness). And automatism, as one of the paths that this object continues to follow, invariably leads to an over-signification of man in his formal essence and in his unconscious desires – thus setting up an obstinate barrier to

5. Indeed, to some extent this still holds good for mechanical objects. The automobile, for example, has always continued to be shaped, even in its essential vehicular function, by the image of man. In its silhouette, its forms, its internal organization, its mode of propulsion and its fuel, its development has persistently passed up all sorts of structural possibilities out of respect for the demands of human morphology, behaviour and psychology.

the object's own concrete structural goal, which is 'to change life'.

Man, for his part, by automating his objects and rendering them multifunctional instead of striving to structure his practices in a fluid and open-ended manner, reveals in a way what part he himself plays in a technical society: that of the most beautiful all-purpose object, that of an instrumental model.

In this sense automatism and personalization do not contradict one another in the slightest. Automatism is simply personalization dreamt in terms of the object. It is the most finished, the most sublime form of the inessential – of that marginal differentiation which subtends man's personalized relationship to his objects.[6]

Functional Aberration: Gadgets

Automatism *per se* is simply a technical deviation, but it opens the door to a whole world of functional delusion, to the entire range of manufactured objects in which a role is played by irrational complexity, obsessive detail, eccentric technicity or gratuitous formalism. In this poly-, para-, hyper- and meta-functional sphere, the object, at its farthest remove from objective determinants, is completely taken over by the imaginary. We have seen that automatism always embodies an irrational projection of consciousness; in this 'schizofunctional' world, however, nothing leaves a trace except obsessions pure and simple. There is a complete pataphysics of the object awaiting description here, a science of imaginary technical solutions.

If we ask, apropos of the objects that surround us, what is structural and what is astructural about them, or if we ask to what extent they are technical objects and to what extent accessories, gadgets or merely formal markers, we shall soon

6. On personalization, see 'Models and Series' below. Automatism is deeply implicated, moreover, in the motivations of fashion and the calculations of production: even the tiniest of increments in the degree of automatism is the surest way to decategorize entire classes of objects.

conclude – our highly neo-technical environment notwithstanding – that we live in a largely rhetorical and allegorical atmosphere. Indeed, it is the baroque, with its predilection for the allegorical, its new discursive individualism based on redundant forms and tricked-up materials, and its demiurgic formalism, that is the true inaugurating moment of the modern age. The baroque clearly foreshadows on the artistic plane all the themes and myths of our technological civilization, right down to its paroxysmic formalism of detail and movement.

Once this point is reached, the technical balance of objects is upset. Too many accessory functions are introduced from the point of view of which *the object answers no need other than the need to function*; it answers, in other words, to the functional superstition according to which for any operation there is – there must be – a corresponding object, and if none exists then one must be invented. As in the tinkering tradition of the Concours Lépine,[7] no true innovation is to be seen, but by juggling stereotyped techniques objects are created that are at once incredibly specific in their function and absolutely useless. So precise is the function proposed, in fact, that it can only be a pretext: such objects are *subjectively* functional, that is to say, obsessional. As for the opposite, 'aesthetic', approach, which omits function altogether and exalts the beauty of pure mechanism, this ultimately amounts to the same thing. For the inventor at the Concours Lépine, the creation of a solar-powered boiled-egg opener or some other equally dotty gadget is merely an excuse for obsessive manipulation and contemplation. Like all obsessions, moreover, this particular variety has its poetic side, as manifested to a greater or lesser degree in Picabia's machines, in Tinguely's mechanical constructions, in the simple clockwork of a discarded watch, or in any object whose original use we simply cannot remember but whose mechanism still arouses a sort of delighted fascination in us.

7. [*Translator's note*: The annual exhibition of the Association of French Inventors and Manufacturers, founded in 1902 by Louis Lépine.]

Something that serves no purpose whatsoever may in this sense still serve *us*.

Pseudo-Functionality: Gizmos

This empty functionalism is well summed up by the word 'gizmo'.[8] A gizmo does have an operational value, but whereas the function of a machine is explicit in its name, a gizmo, in the context of the functional paradigm, is always an indeterminate term with, in addition, the pejorative connotation of 'the thing without a name' or 'the thing I cannot name' (there is something immoral about an object whose exact purpose one does not know). The fact remains that it *works*. As a sort of dangling parenthesis, as an object detached from its function, what the 'gizmo' or the 'thingummyjig' suggests is a vague and limitless functionality – or perhaps better the mental picture of an imaginary functionality.

It would be impossible to classify the whole range of obsessional polyfunctionality. From Marcel Aymé's '*vistemboir*', whose nature is a mystery to everyone, though everyone is sure it does have a use, to that 'Something' which in the Radio Luxembourg guessing game is the subject of endless questions whereby thousands of listeners try to find the name of some minute item (e.g. the strip made of a special stainless alloy that is fitted in a slide trombone which ensures that . . . etc., etc.), and from Sunday-afternoon pottering to James Bond-style super-gadgetry, there extends a panoply of wondrous accessories culminating in the immense industrial output of everyday objects – gadgets or gizmos – whose obsessional degree of specialization easily matches the old-fashioned baroque imagination of the amateur inventor. What is one to say of the ultrasound washing-up machine which removes encrusted food from dishes without the intervention of the human

8. [*Translator's note*: I have used 'gizmo' for the French catch-all term '*machin*', whose close kinship to the French '*machine*' is thus not apparent in the English.]

hand, the toaster with a nine-level browning control, or the electric cocktail swizzle-stick? At the serial and industrial level, what was once merely charming eccentricity or individual neurosis becomes a daily and ceaseless assault on the mind, which is either overtaken by panic or over-excited by sheer detail.

It is frightening to consider just how many things fall into the category of gizmos, just how many of our objects are covered by this empty concept. It is not difficult to see that the proliferation of technical detail here corresponds in each of us to an immense conceptual failure, and that our language is a very long way indeed behind the structures and functional articulation of the objects that we use, as it were, naturally. Our civilization has more and more objects and fewer and fewer names for them. The word 'machine', in becoming applicable to the realm of social labour, has acquired a precise enough generic sense; as recently as the late eighteenth century, however, it had much the same meaning as 'gizmo' today. Words like 'gizmo' now cover all those things which, on account of their specialization and because they answer to no true collective need, cannot be referred to as machines, and thus assume a mythological character. If 'machine' belongs to the sphere of functional 'language', 'gizmo' belongs to the subjective sphere of 'speech'. It goes without saying that in a civilization where such unnameable objects (or at any rate objects designated only in the loosest way, by means of neologism or paraphrase) are multiplying, resistance to mythology is perforce far weaker than in civilizations whose objects are clearly known and denominated down to their most detailed aspects. Today we live in a world of what Georges Friedmann calls Sunday drivers – people who have never opened the bonnets of their cars, people for whom *functioning is not merely the function of things but also their mystery.*

If we grant that our environment, and by extension our everyday view of the world, is thus largely shaped by functional simulacra, we are bound to ask what superstition serves to maintain and compensate for this conceptual inadequacy. What exactly is the key to this mysterious functioning of objects? The answer is a vague but tenacious obsession with a world-machine, with a universal mechanism. The machine and the gizmo are mutually exclusive. It is not that the machine is a perfected form, nor that the gizmo is a degraded one: rather, the two are different in kind, the first operating in the real, the second in the imaginary realm. 'Machine' signifies, and in so doing structures, a particular real practical whole; 'gizmo' signifies nothing more than a *formal* operation – though that operation is the *total* operation of the world. The virtue of a gizmo may be ridiculous in reality,[9] but in the imagination it is universal. The electrical whatsit that extracts stones from fruit or some new vacuum-cleaner accessory for getting under sideboards are perhaps in the end not especially practical, but they do serve to reinforce the belief that for every need there is a possible mechanical answer, that every practical (and even psychological) problem may be foreseen, forestalled, resolved in advance by means of a technical object that is rational and adapted – perfectly adapted. As for what exactly it is adapted to, that is of no consequence. The important thing is that the world should present the appearance of having already been 'operated on'. The real referent of the gizmo is not a plum stone or the narrow space under the sideboard, but nature in its entirety reinvented in accordance with the technical reality principle: a total simulacrum of an automated nature. This is its myth and its mystery. And like all mythologies, this one too has two sides to it: it mystifies man by submerging him in a functional dream, but it equally well mystifies the object by submerging it in the irrationality of human determinants. There is a close collusion between the human-all-too-human and the functional-all-too-functional: the impregnation of the human world by technical goals invariably implies technology's impregnation by human ones – for better or for worse. We are, however, far more sensitive to human relationships being interfered with by the absurd and totalitarian concerns

9. A minimal practical impingement on reality is nevertheless always required as a justification for the imaginary projection involved here.

of technology than we are to technological development being interfered with by the absurd and totalitarian concerns of human beings. Yet it is unquestionably human irrationality and its figments which fuel the tendency for any machine to take on gizmo-like properties; it is they, in other words, which agitate functional *phantasy* behind any concrete functional *praxis*.

The true functionality of the gizmo is unconscious in character – hence its fascination for us. That it should be absolutely functional, absolutely adapted (though to what?), shows that this functionality and this adaptation must needs refer to a demand of a non-practical kind. The myth of a wonder-working functionality of the *world* is correlated with the phantasy of a wonder-working functionality of the *body*. There is a direct link between the paradigm of technical action executed by the world and the paradigm of sexual action executed by the subject; and in this perspective the gizmo, the ultimate tool, is basically a substitute for the phallus, the operative medium of function *par excellence*. Moreover, any object has something of the gizmo about it, for in proportion as its practical instrumentality fades it becomes susceptible of cathexis by a libidinal instrumentality. This is already true of the child's toy, or of any stone or piece of wood as perceived by 'primitives'; as we have seen, 'uncivilized' people can fetishize a simple pen, and 'civilized' ones can do the same with absolutely any abandoned mechanical object or ancient artefact.

For any object whatsoever, in fact, the reality principle may be put in brackets. *No sooner does an object lose its concrete practical aspect than it is transferred to the realm of mental practices.* In short, behind every real object there is a dream object.

We have already discussed the case of antiques in this context. In their case, however, the transcendence or mental abstraction concerned the material or the form, and was bound up with a regressive birth complex; pseudo-functional objects or 'gizmos', by contrast, are bound up with an abstract transcendence of the object's *functioning*, and hence with a projective, phallic power complex. Let me stress once more that this is an analytic distinction: whereas objects normally have but one real function, narrowly defined, their 'mental' functionality is unlimited, and any number of phantasies may have a place therein. A distinct evolution in their imaginary aspect is nevertheless signalled by the shift from an animistic to an energetic structure: traditional objects tended to bear witness to our *presence*, being static symbols of our bodily organs, but technical objects hold a different kind of fascination in that they evoke a virtual *energy*, and are thus less receptacles of our presence than vehicles of our dynamic self-image. Here too, moreover, a reservation is called for, because the operation of energy itself tends to be down-played in the most modern devices, with their encapsulated and elliptical forms. In a world dominated by communications and information, the sight of energy at work has become a rarity. Miniaturization and gestural depletion erode symbolic expressiveness.[10] But we may take comfort in the fact that even if objects sometimes escape practical human control, they never escape the imagination. *Modes of the imaginary follow modes of technological evolution*, and it is therefore to be expected that the next mode of technical efficiency will give rise to a new imaginary mode. At present its traits are difficult to discern, but perhaps, in the wake of the animistic and energetic modes, we shall need to turn our attention to the structures of a cybernetic imaginary mode whose central myth will no longer be that of an absolute organicism, nor that of an absolute functionalism, but instead that of an absolute interrelatedness of the world. For the time being our everyday environment remains unevenly divided between the three. The old sideboard, the car and the tape recorder exist side by side in the one sphere, even though their imaginary modes of existence, just like their technical modes of existence, differ radically.

10. In a world of miniaturized, mute, unmediated and impeccable appliances, the automobile, thanks to the dramatic visibility of engine and controls, remains the great exception – and the spectacular object *par excellence*.

At all events, whatever the functioning of the object may be like, we invariably experience it as OUR functioning: whatever the object's efficient mode – even should it be absurd, as in the case of the 'gizmo' – we project ourselves into that efficiency. In fact we do so *especially* when it is absurd, as witness the old phrase, at once magical and comical, according to which a thing 'might always come in useful': while it is true that objects do indeed serve specific purposes at times, they are much more commonly good for everything and nothing, and in that case their true utility lies in the very fact that they 'might always come in useful'.

Metafunctionality: Robots

The ultimate expression of such imaginary projection is the object as dreamt up by science fiction – the pure realm of the gizmo. We should be greatly mistaken were we to view science fiction as an escape from everyday reality: on the contrary, it is an extrapolation from the irrational tendencies of that reality through the free exercise of narrative invention. Although it is an invaluable witness to the civilization of the object, precisely because it heightens certain aspects thereof, science fiction has absolutely no prophetic value. It has practically nothing to do with the real future of technological development, for which it accounts in the future perfect tense, so to speak, drawing for nourishment on sublime archaisms and on a repertory of acquired forms and functions. It contains little in the way of structural invention, but it is an inexhaustible mine of imaginary solutions to stereotyped needs and functional requirements of an often marginal or mind-boggling variety. In a way science fiction is the apotheosis of tinkering. But while its true exploratory value may be very feeble, it supplies us with a wealth of information on the unconscious.

In particular, science fiction demonstrates what we have re-cognized as the most profound – albeit the most irrational – feature of the modern object, namely its automatism. When it comes down to it, the genre has only ever invented one super-object: the ROBOT. Soon man will no longer even have to steer his lawnmower on a Sunday afternoon, because it will start itself up, and stop once the job is done, of its own accord. Is this the only conceivable fate of objects? The itinerary laid down for them, leading inexorably to the complete automation of their existing functions,[11] has far less to do with humanity's future technology than with its present psychological motivations. Consequently, the myth of the robot may be said to cover all paths taken by the unconscious in the realm of objects. The robot is a symbolic microcosm of both man and the world, which is to say that it simultaneously replaces both man and the world, synthesizing absolute functionality and absolute anthropomorphism. Its ante-cedents were electrical household appliances (cf. the 'automatic maid'). Fundamentally, therefore, the robot is simply the mytho-logical end-product of a naïve phase of the imagination, a phase which implies the projection of a continual and *visible* function-ality. For the substitution in question has to be visible: if it is to exert its fascination without creating insecurity, the robot must unequivocally reveal its nature as a mechanical prosthesis (its body is metallic, its gestures are discrete, jerky and unhuman). A robot that mimicked man to the point where its gestures had a truly human fluidity would create anxiety. What the robot must be is the symbol of a world at once entirely functionalized and entirely

11. And perhaps – who knows? – to the total mimetism of 'spontaneous' self-generation, with coffee mills giving birth to baby coffee mills, just as children imagine. But things could surely then go no farther, because a machine capable of manufacturing an identical machine is, strictly speaking, inconceivable. Such a situation would clearly represent the ultimate in autonomy (a logic which always ends in tautology), but it is a situation that the imaginary realm cannot embrace, because that would mean also embracing magical and infantile regression back to a stage where automatic duplication or scissiparity is possible. Such a machine would in any case be the height of absurdity: self-reproduction being its sole function, it could never pod peas at the same time. . . . Reproduction is never the sole function of man himself. The imaginary is not synonymous with madness, and it must always effectively preserve the distinction between man and his double.

personalized, and hence reassuring at all levels; a world which can reincarnate the abstracted power of man just as far as is conceivable short of its being utterly engulfed by identification.[12]

If, for the unconscious, the robot is the perfect object that sums up all the others, this is not simply because it is a simulacrum of man as a functionally efficient being; rather, it is because, though the robot is indeed such a simulacrum, it is not so perfect in this regard as to be man's double, and because, for all its humanness, it always remains quite visibly an object, and hence a *slave*. In the last analysis, robots are always slaves. They may be endowed with any of the qualities that define human sovereignty except one, and that is sex. Their fascination and their symbolic value must operate under this one constraint. By virtue of their multifunctionalism they attest to man's phallic reign over the world, but at the same time, inasmuch as they are controlled, dominated, directed and rendered asexual, they also attest to a phallus that is enslaved, to a sexuality that is domesticated and unaccompanied by anxiety: all that remains is an obedient functionality embodied (so to speak) in an object which resembles me, an object to which the world is subject yet which is simultaneously subject to my will. In this way a threatening part of myself has been exorcized and turned into a sort of all-powerful slave, cast in my image, which I can use for purposes of self-aggrandizement.

It is thus not hard to understand the urge that exists to have all objects accede to the status of robots. This is the logical end of the

12. Let me return here for a moment to the fable of the eighteenth-century automaton that I recounted above (see p. 56). When the illusionist, at the pinnacle of his artistry, renders his own gestures mechanical and subtly changes his own appearance, his intention is to bring out his performance's true *raison d'être*, which is the pleasure to be derived from the difference between the automaton and the man. His audience would be far too alarmed if they were really unable to tell which figure was 'real', and he knows full well that creating a perfect automaton, and hence a perfect identity, is far less important than giving play to difference – and, indeed, that the very best outcome is that the spectators should take the machine for the man and the man for the machine.

object's unconscious psychological function. Its *actual* end, too – for the robot can evolve no farther: *it is frozen in its resemblance to man* and in functional abstraction at all costs. Active genital sexuality expires here also, because, as projected into the robot, it is neutralized, deactivated, conjured away – itself immobilized within the object whose development it has terminated. The process of abstraction here is narcissistic; the universe of science fiction is asexual.

The robot is interesting on a number of other counts also. As the mythological end of the object, it gathers unto itself all the phantasies attendant upon our deepest relationships with our environment.

The robot is a slave, then, but let us not forget that the theme of slavery is always bound up – even in the legend of the sorcerer's apprentice – with the theme of *revolt*. In one form or another, robots in revolt are by no means rare in science fiction. And that revolt is implicit even when it is not manifest. The robot, like the slave, is both good and perfidious: good as a captive force; perfidious as a force that may break its chains. Like the sorcerer's apprentice, man has every reason to fear the resurrection of this force which he has exorcized and bound to his own image. It is in fact his own sexuality, liable now to turn against him, that he is afraid of. Once liberated, unchained and in revolt, sexuality becomes man's mortal enemy. This is the lesson of the frequent and unpredictable revolts of robots, of the maleficent mutations that affect them, and even merely of the disquieting, ever-present threat of such brutal conversions occurring. Man is thus prey to the deepest forces within him: he finds himself confronted by a double who has enlisted his energies and whose appearance, according to legend, spells death. What the mechanical perfidy of the science-fiction robot means (beyond the implication of a functional breakdown of the environment) is that subjugated phallic energies are rising in revolt. These narratives propose two solutions in this situation. Sometimes man tames the 'evil' forces that have been unleashed, and 'moral' order is restored.

Alternatively, the forces embodied in the robot self-destruct: automatism is itself driven to suicide. The theme of the robot that goes off the rails and destroys itself is a common one – indeed, it is closely akin to the theme of the robot in revolt. There is a secret apocalypse of objects – or of the Object – which fuels the passionate interest of the reader. It is tempting to connect this development to a moral denunciation of the diabolical nature of science, the point being that if technology is on its own road to damnation, man will be restored to an untrammelled nature. This moral theme unquestionably plays a part in fictional narratives, but it is at once too naïve and too rational. Morality *per se* fascinates no one, yet the anticipated disintegration of the robot produces a strange satisfaction. The recurrent phantasy of ritualistic fragmentation which is the culminating point of the object's functional triumphalism is determined less by a moral constraint than by a profound wish. The spectacle of death is relished, and if we accept the idea that the robot symbolizes a subjugated sexuality, then by extension the robot's disintegration must constitute for man the symbolic spectacle of the atomization of his own sexuality – which he himself destroys, having pressed it into the service of his image. If we carry the Freudian view to its logical conclusion, we cannot but wonder whether this is not man's way of using technology in its most demented incarnations to celebrate the future occurrence of his own death, his way of renouncing his sexuality in order to be quit of all anxiety.

The current fashion for 'happenings' has brought the great science-fiction event of the 'suicide' or murder of the object a little closer to home. The happening involves an orgiastic destruction and debasement of objects, a veritable hecatomb whereby our whole satiated culture revels in its own degradation and death. A recent fad in the United States amounts to a mass-marketing of the happening in the shape of novel contraptions, composed of gears, rods, shafts and what-have-you – true jewels of useless functionality whose merit lies in the fact that they fall apart of their own accord, suddenly and irreparably, after a few hours of operation.

These objects are exchanged as gifts, and the period during which they duly malfunction, disintegrate and die is the occasion for a social get-together.

A similar, though less extreme, phenomenon is the embodiment in certain present-day objects of a kind of *fatum*. Here the car once again has pride of place. The individual commits himself to a car for better or for worse. Certainly the car serves him, but he would seem to accept and expect something more from it: the sort of destiny which in the cinema, for example, is ritually represented by death in a road accident.

The Transformations of Technology

We may thus trace functional mythologies, born of technics itself, all the way to a sort of fatality in which the world-mastering technology seems to crystallize in the form of an inverse and threatening purpose. At this point it behoves us to do two things. In the first place, we must reframe the problem of the fragility of objects, and of their defection; for although in the first instance objects present themselves to us as reassuring, as factors of equilibrium, albeit of a neurotic kind, they are also in the end a factor of continual disillusionment. Secondly, we must challenge our society's implicit assumption that a rationality of ends and means governs the sphere of production and the technological project itself.

The object's dysfunctionality, its counter-purpose, is governed by two parallel sets of determinants: a socio-economic system of production and a psychological system of projection. It is the reciprocal involvement of these two systems, their collusion, that we need to define.

Technological society thrives on a tenacious myth, the myth of uninterrupted technical progress accompanied by a continuing moral 'backwardness' of man relative thereto. These two claims are mutually supportive: moral 'stagnation' transfigures technical progress and turns it into the only certain value, and hence the ultimate authority of our society; by the same token, the system of production is absolved of all responsibility. A supposed moral contradiction serves to conceal the true contradiction, which is the fact, precisely, that the present production system, while working for real technological progress, at the same time opposes it (along with any restructuring of social relationships to which it might lead). The myth of a happy convergence of technology, production and consumption masks all political and economic counterpurposes. How indeed could a system of techniques and objects conceivably progress harmoniously while the system of relations between the people who produced it continued to stagnate or regress? The fact is that humans and their techniques, needs and objects are structurally interlocked come what may. The indivisibility, within any single cultural sphere, of individual and social structures and of technical and functional modalities must surely be deemed axiomatic. Our technological civilization is no exception to the rule: techniques and objects therein suffer the same servitudes as human beings – and the process of material organization, hence of objective technical progress, is subject to exactly the same blocks, deviations and regressions as the concrete process of the socialization of human relationships, hence of objective social progress.

There is a cancer of the object: the proliferation of astructural elements that underpins the object's triumphalism is a kind of cancer. It is upon such astructural elements (automatism, accessory features, inessential differences) that the entire social network of fashion and controlled consumption is founded.[13] They are the bulwark which tends to halt genuine technical development. On their account, while appearing to manifest all the metamorphic powers of a prodigious health, objects that are already saturated wear themselves out completely through convulsive formal variation and changes whose impact is strictly visual. 'Technically speaking,' writes Lewis Mumford, 'changes in form and style are

13. See 'Models and Series' below.

signs of immaturity; they mark a period of transition. The error of capitalism as a creed lies in the attempt to make this period of transition a permanent one.'[14] And Mumford notes that in the United States, for example, after the grand wave of inventions which between 1910 and 1940 brought in the automobile, the aeroplane, the refrigerator, the television, and so on, significant invention practically petered out. Improvement, refinement, packaging – anything to enhance the prestige of the object, but nothing by way of structural innovation. 'The chief obstacle to the fuller development of the machine lies in the association of taste and fashion with waste and commercial profiteering.'[15] On the one hand, indeed, minor improvements, added complexity and ancillary systems sustain a false consciousness of 'progress' and conceal the urgent necessity for fundamental changes (a 'reformism' of the object, one might say). On the other hand, fashion – which, with its inchoate proliferation of secondary systems, is ruled by chance – is also the realm of an infinite recurrence of forms, and hence of maximum commercial prospects. There is in fact a fundamental antagonism between the verticality of technology and the horizontality of profit – between the continual self-transcendence of technical invention and the closedness of a system of recurrent objects and forms beholden to the goals of production.

This is where we encounter the ambition of objects to act as replacements for human relationships. In its concrete function the object solves a practical problem, but *in its inessential aspects it resolves a social or psychological conflict*. Such, at any rate, is the modern 'philosophy' of the object as understood by Ernest Dichter, prophet of motivation research, whose thesis boils down

14. *Technics and Civilization* (see above, p. 57, note 37), p. 396. The decisiveness of capitalism in this regard is manifest for an entire period, certainly, but once a certain threshold in technological development and in the distribution of goods and products has been passed, things are far less cut and dried.
15. Ibid., p. 353.

to the claim that for any source of tension whatsoever, for any individual or collective conflict, there must be an object capable of resolving it.[16] Just as there is a saint for every day of the year, so there is an object for every problem: the important thing is to manufacture and launch that object at the right moment. What Dichter deems an ideal solution, however, Mumford more accurately sees as a solution by default, but Mumford's conception of the object and of technics as substitute answers to human conflicts – a conception which he extends within a critical perspective to our whole civilization – is essentially the same as Dichter's. 'The fact is', he writes,

> that an elaborate mechanical organization is often a temporary and expensive substitute for an effective social organization or for a sound biological adaptation.

> Power machines have given a sort of licence to social inefficiency.

> The machine, so far from being a sign in our present civilization of human power and order, is often an indication of ineptitude and social paralysis.[17]

It is difficult to assess the total cost to society as a whole of thus referring real conflicts and needs to the technical sphere, itself in thrall to fashion and forced consumption. But that cost is certainly colossal. If one considers the automobile, for instance, it is very hard now even to imagine what an extraordinary tool for the reorganization of human relations it might have been, thanks to its victory over space and the structural convergence of several techniques that it represented, so quickly did it become encrusted with parasitic functions defined by the requirements of prestige,

16. See *The Strategy of Desire* (Garden City, NY: Doubleday, 1960), p. 84.
17. Mumford, *Technics*, pp. 275, 276 and 426 respectively.

comfort, unconscious projection, and so forth – functions which first impeded and then blocked the automobile's essential function, which was human integration. Today the car is a completely inert object. Ever more thoroughly abstracted from its social function of transportation, while at the same time serving to trap that function within archaic modalities, it continues to undergo frantic transformations, revisions and metamorphoses within the limits of possibility of a structure that cannot be changed. And a whole civilization can come to a halt in the same way as the automobile.

Three collateral lines of development may be distinguished here. The first concerns the technical structuring of the object, implying the convergence of functions, integration, material form and economy. The second concerns a parallel structuring of the world and of nature: space is mastered, energy is controlled, materials are mobilized – and a more meaningful and interrelated world emerges. Thirdly, human praxis, both individual and collective, is so structured as to foster an ever greater 'relativity' and mobility, along with an open-ended integration and an 'economy' of society analogous to that of the most highly evolved technical objects. Despite the discrepancies arising from the distinct dynamics of each of these levels, it may be observed that, broadly speaking, whenever development slows or stops, it does so on all three at once. Once a technical object's development is arrested at a given outcome (which at the second level, in the case of the car, means a *partial* victory over space), it will henceforward do no more than continue to connote that frozen structure, to which all manner of subjective motivations will now return cathectically (regression at the third level). It is at this point that the technical object, having lost all dynamism, may enter into a relationship of fixed complementarity: car and house, for example, will come to constitute a closed system invested with conventional values, and the car, ceasing to serve relationship or exchange, will truly be nothing but an object of consumption: 'Not alone have the older forms of technics served to constrain the development of the neotechnic economy: but the new inventions and devices have been frequently used to maintain, renew, and stabilize the structure of the old order.'[18] The automobile no longer removes obstacles between men; on the contrary, men now invest the automobile with that which separates them. Space mastered becomes an even greater obstacle than the space over which mastery was sought in the first place.[19]

Technics and the Unconscious System

All the same, we have eventually to ask ourselves whether there is not something more at the root of this relative stagnation of forms and techniques, this systematic deficit (whose remarkable efficiency in terms of social integration will nevertheless be confirmed below when we discuss 'Models and Series'), than the self-interested dictatorship of a system of production, than an absolutely – and absolutely alienating – social agency. Whether, as Lewis Mumford puts it, it is simply a 'social accident' that objects remain in a state of underdevelopment. If humanity were 'innocent' in this respect, if the production system alone were responsible for technology's immaturity, there would indeed be an accident here – a contradiction just as inexplicable as its diametrical opposite, the bourgeois fiction of 'advanced' technol-

18. Ibid., p. 266.
19. In a comparable way we may suppose that cinema and television have passed up, or are in the midst of passing up, vast concrete opportunities for 'changing life'. As Edgar Morin has written:

> Nobody is surprised by the fact that from the instant of its birth the cinematograph was drastically diverted from its apparent technical and scientific goals, that it was snapped up by show business and turned into the 'cinema', with the result that developments that might have seemed natural were atrophied from the outset. (*Le cinéma ou l'homme imaginaire* [Paris: Editions de Minuit, 1956], p. 15)

Morin goes on to show how the sluggishness of innovation (sound, colour, depth) was bound up with the consumption-driven exploitation of the cinema.

ogy held back by moral 'retardation'. The truth is that there is no accident, and even if we must assign the lion's share of responsibility to a production system, structurally linked to the social order, which exploits the entire society by means of a system of objects, we still cannot help concluding, in view of the system's permanence and solidity, that a collusion exists somewhere between the collective order of production and an individual order of needs, albeit an unconscious one. What I mean by 'collusion' is a close relationship of negative complicity, or a set of reciprocal determinations, between the dysfunctionality of the socio-economic system and the far-reaching effects of the unconscious; the question was touched on above in connection with robots.

If connotation and personalization, fashion and automatism, all tend to focus upon those astructural features whose irrational motivations the logic of production seeks to control and systematize, this is perhaps also because man has neither a clear will to transcend nor any great prospect of transcending the aforementioned archaic structures of projection; or at least that he has a deep-seated resistance to sacrificing subjective, projective virtualities and their eternal recurrence on the altar of concrete structural development (both technical and social); or again, to put it in the simplest terms, that man has a profound resistance to imposing rationality upon the purely arbitrary goals of his needs. This may well constitute a fatal turn for the *modus existendi* of the object, as indeed of society as a whole. Once a certain point in technical development has been reached, and once primary needs have been satisfied, we may well demand a phantasied, allegorical and subconscious edibility of the object as much as, or even more than, an actual functionality. Why is it, after all, that the design of the automobile is not different: why is the driver's seat not positioned forward and the vehicle streamlined in such a way as to let the operator efficiently occupy the space he has to travel through, instead of placing him in a substitute house – even, as it were, within a substitute subject endowed with projectile force? Surely the answer must be that the current form (even more exaggerated in racing cars, whose excessively long bonnet has every appearance of providing an absolute *model* here) facilitates an essential projection which is ultimately far more important than any progress in the art and science of travel.

Apparently man needs to overburden the world with this 'unconscious' discourse of his, even at the cost of halting that world's development. The implications of this are very far-reaching. If indeed the astructural elements around which our most tenacious desires seem to crystallize are not just parallel functions, complications or overloads, but properly speaking dysfunctions, failures or aberrations relative to an objective structural order, if indeed a whole civilization appears ready to turn away on their account from a genuine revolution in its structures, and if indeed all this is not accidental, then we are justified in asking whether man, under cover of the myth of functional extravagance (or 'personalized affluence'), which in fact conceals an obsession with his own image, does not after all incline much more towards an increasingly dysfunctional world than towards an increasingly functional one. He does appear, at any rate, to go along with the play of dysfunctions which is progressively turning our environment into a world of objects arrested in their growth by their own outgrowths, as it were, objects disappointed and disappointing to the very extent that they become personalized.

The substitutional aspect of the object, which a moment ago we noted was a decisive one, is even more in evidence here: it is even truer on the plane of unconscious conflicts than on that of social or conscious psychological ones, as evoked by Ernest Dichter and Lewis Mumford, that the use of technics – and, more simply, the consumption of objects – has secondary roles to play, imaginary solutions to offer. Technics as an effective mediation between man and the world is indeed the harder path. The easier path is the interpolation of a system of objects as an imaginary resolution of contradictions of every kind. This amounts to a short circuit between the technical order and the order of individual needs, a short circuit which exhausts the energies of both systems. Small wonder that the resulting system of objects should bear the stigma of defection: its structural deficiency reflects the contradiction to which the system offers a merely formal solution. As the individual or collective *cover* for one conflict or another, the system of objects is inevitably marked by its denial of those conflicts.

But what are the conflicts that objects are called upon to cover up? Humanity has its whole future wagered on the simultaneous harnessing of natural external forces and of the internal pressure of the libido, both of which it experiences as threatening and fateful. The unconscious economy of the system of objects is a mechanism of projection and domestication (or control) of the libido which brings an efficient principle to bear. The domination of nature and the production of goods are in effect a parallel benefit thereof. Unfortunately, however, this admirable economy carries a dual risk for the human order: first there is the danger that sexuality might be in some sense conjured away and foreclosed in the technical realm, secondly the danger that this technical realm might in turn be disturbed in its development by the conflicted energy by which it has been invested. All the preconditions are thus assembled for the emergence of an insoluble contradiction, a permanent defection: the fact is that the system of objects as it operates today embodies an ever-present potential for *consent* to this sort of regression – the lure of an end to sexuality, its definitive absorption in the recurrence and continual forward flight of the technical order.

In practice the technical order always retains a certain dynamism of its own that blocks the sort of infinite recurrence characteristic of a perfect regressive system of this kind (which is equivalent, strictly speaking, to death). The necessary conditions for such an eventuality are nevertheless present in our system of objects, and the system is *haunted by the temptation of a reverse evolution which coexists in it with the potential for progress.*

This temptation to regress towards what can only be called death as a way of escaping from sexual anxiety sometimes assumes forms – still within the context of the technical order – that are ever more spectacular and brutal. It may then be transformed into the temptation, truly tragic in its implications, to see this order itself turned against its instigator – that is, against humanity; to see an ineluctable fate re-emerge from within the very technical order that had been designed to exorcize it – a process akin to the one described by Freud, whereby repressed energy returns via the repressing agency itself and derails all mechanisms of defence. In contrast to the reassurance vouchsafed by a gradual regression, the tragic variety precipitates the dizzying sensations associated with such a brusque resolution of the conflict between the sexual drives and the ego. These sensations are a response to the eruption of hitherto contained energies within technical objects themselves – that is to say, within the very symbols of mastery over the world. Two contradictory goals are pursued simultaneously: the inevitability of fate is challenged, yet at the same time sought. This contradiction is reflected in the economic order of production, which, though it produces ceaselessly, can produce only fragile objects – objects that are partly dysfunctional and destined for an early death; the system thus works to destroy such objects as well as to produce them.

Let me stress once again that it is not the fragility of objects that is tragic, nor their death. Rather, it is the *temptation* represented by that fragility and that death. This temptation is satisfied in a way when an object fails us, even though this failing may at the same time inconvenience us or throw us into despair. This is the same kind of malign and vertiginous satisfaction that we encountered earlier, as projected into phantasies of revolt and destruction on the part of robots. The object takes its revenge. It becomes 'personalized' – in this case for the worse – because it revolts. This hostile volte-face may shock us and take us by surprise, but there is no denying that a submissive attitude soon develops towards this revolt, which we treat as inevitable, and as evidence of a fragility that distinctly appeals to us. A technical hitch infuriates us, but an avalanche of technical hitches can fill us with glee; if a jug develops a crack we are pained, but if it smashes to smithereens there is satisfaction in it. Our reaction to an object's failure is in fact always ambiguous. *This failure threatens our well-being, yet it gives material expression to the objection that we continually raise with respect to ourselves – an objection which also demands satisfaction.* As Ernest Dichter points out, you expect a cigarette lighter to work, but 'you do not assume, or even desire, that your lighter would admirably perform under all conditions'.[20] One has merely to imagine an infallible object, and the disillusion it would inevitably entail in connection – precisely – with the aforementioned objection one has to oneself, in order to realize that infallibility invariably generates anxiety. The fact is that a world without fallibility would imply the definitive resorption of an inevitable fate – and hence of sexuality. This is why we greet the slightest hint of a resurgence of fatefulness with deep satisfaction: the slightest breach allows sexuality to revive, even if for only a moment, even if it takes the form of a hostile force (as it always does in this context), and even if its emergence in such circumstances means failure, death and destruction. The underlying contradiction is thus resolved in contradictory fashion, but could things really go otherwise?[21]

Our 'technological' civilization, as foreshadowed by the American model, is a world at once systematized and fragile. The system of objects is the embodiment of this systematization of fragility, of ephemerality, of the ever more rapid recurrence of the repetition compulsion; the embodiment of satisfaction and disillusion; the embodiment of the problematical exorcism of the real conflicts

20. Dichter, *The Strategy of Desire*, p. 94.
21. A good illustration of this is the legend of the Student of Prague, according to which the protagonist's image steps out of the mirror and assumes the form of a double which haunts him (following the conclusion of a pact with the devil). Henceforward he has no reflection in the mirror, though his image continues to haunt him. One day, when the double happens (as in the primal scene) to be standing between him and the mirror, the student shoots and kills it – which is to say, of course, that he kills himself, for the double has stripped him of his reality. Just before he dies, however, he rediscovers his true image in the shards of the broken mirror.

that threaten individual and social relationships. With the advent of our consumer society, we are seemingly faced for the first time in history by an irreversible organized attempt to swamp society with objects and integrate it into an indispensable system designed to replace all open interaction between natural forces, needs and techniques. The principal basis of this system would appear to be the official, obligatory and supervised demise of the objects that it comprises: a gigantic collective 'happening' whereby the death of the group itself is celebrated through the euphoric destruction or ritualistic devouring of objects and gestures.[22] Here again one could argue that nothing more is involved than an infantile disorder of the technological society, and attribute such growing pains entirely to the dysfunctionality of our present social structures – i.e. to the capitalist order of production. The long-term prospect of a transcendence of the whole system would thus remain open. On the other hand, if something more is involved than the anarchic ends of a production system determined by social exploitation, if deeper conflicts in fact play a part – highly individual conflicts, but extended onto the collective plane – then any prospect of ultimate transcendence must be abandoned for ever. Are we contemplating the developmental problems of a society ultimately destined to become the best of all possible worlds, or, alternatively, an organized regression in the face of insoluble problems? Is all this the work of anarchic production relations or of the death instinct? What, in short, has made a civilization go wrong in this way? The question is still open.

22. This is what Edgar Morin has called the nihilism of consumption.

D. The socio-ideological system of objects and their consumption

I Models and Series

The Pre-Industrial Object and the Industrial Model

The status of the modern object is dominated by the MODEL/SERIES distinction. To some extent, things were ever thus. A privileged minority in society has always served as a testing-ground for successive styles whose solutions, methods and artifices were then disseminated by local craftsmen. All the same, one cannot exactly speak of 'models' or 'series' in connection with any time before the industrial era. For one thing, there was a far greater homogeneity among all objects in pre-industrial society, because the mode of their production was still everywhere handcraft, because they were far less specialized in function, and because the cultural range of forms was more restricted (there being little reference to earlier or to extraneous traditions); furthermore, there was a much tighter segregation between the class of objects that could lay claim to 'style' and the class of locally produced objects that had use value only. Today a farmhouse table has cultural value, but just thirty years ago its sole value arose from the purpose it served. In the eighteenth century there was simply no relationship between a 'Louis XV' table and a peasant's table: there was an unbridgeable gulf between the two types of object, just as there was between the two corresponding social classes. No single cultural system embraced them both.[1] Nor

1. Differences between classes of objects are doubtless never quite so sharp as those between social classes, however. The absolute hierarchical distinction between orders of society is mitigated at the level of objects by use: a table, after all, serves the same basic function at every rung of the social ladder.

can it be said that a Louis XIII table is the model of which the countless tables and chairs that later imitated it are the serial form.[2] A limited dissemination of craft techniques did occur here, but there was no dissemination of *values*: the 'model' remained absolute, for it was bound to a transcendent reality. No serial production in the modern sense could be based on it. The social order was what gave objects their standing. A person was noble or not: nobility was not the ultimate – privileged – term in a series but, rather, a grace that bestowed absolute distinction. In the realm of objects the equivalent of this transcendent idea of nobility is what we call the 'style' of a period.

This distinction between pre-industrial 'period' objects and the 'models' of today is a very important one, because it allows us to get beyond the purely formal opposition and clarify the concrete relationship between model and series in our modern system.

Considering that broad strata of our society do in fact live among serially produced objects that refer formally and psychologically to models which only a small minority can enjoy, there is a strong temptation to simplify the problem by positing a polarity between the former and the latter, and then assigning the value of reality to just one of the poles: to separate series and model completely so as neatly to assign one to the real and the other to the imaginary realm. Unfortunately, the everydayness of serial objects is not unreal as compared with a putative world of models as true values, nor is the sphere of models imaginary just because it affects but a tiny minority, and thus might seem to fall outside social reality. Thanks to mass information and communications systems which promote models, there is now not only a well-established circulation of objects as such but also a 'psychological' circulation which constitutes a radical watershed

---

2. It is true that much more recently the Henri II sideboard has become a true serial object, but this was achieved via the very different route of the industrial production of cultural objects.

between our industrial age and the pre-industrial age of the transcendent distinctiveness of period 'style'. Anyone who has bought a walnut bedroom set at Dubonbois Home Furnishings or a few mass-produced electrical household appliances, and may indeed have done so as a way of realizing a personal dream and as a mark of upward social mobility, knows full well at the same time, through the press, the cinema or the television, that completely 'harmonized' and 'fully functional' living spaces are on the market. Naturally he perceives such things as part of a world of luxury and status from which he is almost inevitably excluded by money; yet he also feels that today this exclusion is no longer underwritten by any class-based legal statute, by any transcending social rationale buttressed by laws. This conviction is of paramount psychological significance, because it means that despite the frustration, despite the material impossibility of acceding to the model object, the use of serial objects invariably embodies an implicit or explicit reference to models.

Reciprocally, models themselves have quit their former isolated, caste-like existence;[3] having become part of industrial production, they are themselves now open to serial distribution. They, too, are now said to be 'functional' (an unthinkable claim for 'period' furniture) and in principle accessible to all. Likewise anyone, in principle, via the very humblest of objects, may partake of the model. Indeed, both model and serial objects in the pure form are increasingly difficult to find. The transition from the one to the other is subject to an infinite differentiation. Just like the production process, the object traverses every shade in the social spectrum. Such transitions are experienced in everyday life in terms of possibility and in terms of frustration: the model is internalized by those who are involved with serial objects, while the series is intimated, negated, transcended and lived in a contradictory

3 This is not to say that they have lost their class-specific character (see below).

manner by those who have to do with models. The socially immanent tendency whereby the series hews ever more narrowly to the model, while the model is continually being diffused into the series, has set up a perpetual dynamic which is in fact the very ideology of our society.

The 'Personalized' Object

It should be noted that the model/series scheme regarding the distribution of objects does not apply evenly to all categories. It works fine in the realm of clothing (for example, a dress from Fath versus a ready-to-wear dress) or in that of cars (for example, a Facel-Vega versus a Citroën 2CV). The more specific an object's function, however, the more ambiguous things become; thus the difference between a 'Frigidaire' from General Motors and a 'Frigeco' refrigerator, or between one television set and another, is not so easy to classify. In the case of small utensils such as coffee mills, the notion of 'model' tends to become indistinguishable from that of 'type', because the object's function tends very largely to absorb differences of status, which may eventually amount to no more than the contrast between luxury models and serial models. (This distinction marks the weakest expression of the notion of model.) At the opposite extreme, when we turn our attention to machines – collective objects *par excellence* – we find that there is no such thing, either, as a luxury version of a pure machine: a rolling-mill, even if it is the only example of its type in the world, is still, from the moment it appears, a serial object. One machine may be more 'modern' than another, but this does not make it the 'model' for which other, less advanced machines constitute the corresponding series. In order to ensure comparable performance, it will be necessary to build other machines of the same type – that is, to construct a pure series on the basis of this first member. There is no place here for a range of calibrated differences that might serve as the basis of a psychological dynamic. At the level of pure function, since there are no combinative variants, there cannot be any models either.[4]

The psycho-sociological dynamic of model and series does not, therefore, operate at the level of the object's primary function, but merely at the level of a secondary function, at the level of the 'personalized' object. That is to say: at the level of an object grounded simultaneously in individual requirements and in that system of differences which is, properly speaking, the cultural system itself.

Choice

No object is proposed to the consumer as a single variety. We may not be granted the material means to buy it, but what our industrial society always offers us 'a priori', as a kind of collective grace and as the mark of a formal freedom, is choice. This availability of the object is the foundation of 'personalization':[5] only if the buyer is offered a whole range of choices can he transcend the strict necessity of his purchase and commit himself *personally* to something beyond it. Indeed, we no longer even have the option of *not* choosing, of buying an object on the sole grounds of its utility, for no object these days is offered for sale on such a 'zero-level' basis. Our freedom to choose causes us to participate in a cultural system willy-nilly. It follows that the choice in question is a specious one: to experience it as freedom is simply to be less sensible of the fact that it is imposed upon us as such, and that through it society as a whole is likewise imposed upon us.

4. The work of art does not answer to the model/series scheme either. The same categorical alternative is posed here as for the machine: the machine fulfils or does not fulfil a function, the work of art is genuine or fake. There are no marginal differences. Only at the level of the private and personalized object (not at the level of the work itself) does the model/series dynamic come into play.
5. Where an object does exist in one version only (as in the case of cars in East Germany), this is an indication of penury which strictly speaking antedates the consumer society. No society can afford to consider such a stage anything but provisional.

Choosing one car over another may perhaps personalize your choice, but the most important thing about the fact of choosing is that it assigns you a place in the overall economic order. According to John Stuart Mill, choosing such and such an object in order to distinguish oneself from other people is in itself of service to society. Increasing the number of objects makes it easier for society to divert the faculty of choice onto them, so neutralizing the threat that the personal demand for choice always represents for it. Clearly 'personalization', far from being a mere advertising ploy, is actually a basic ideological concept of a society which 'personalizes' objects and beliefs solely in order to integrate persons more effectively.[6]

Marginal Difference

The corollary of the fact that every object reaches us by way of a choice is the fact that fundamentally no object is offered as a serial object, that every single object claims model status. The most insignificant object must be marked off by some distinguishing feature – a colour, an accessory, a detail of one sort or another. Such a detail is always presented as specific: 'This dustbin is absolutely original – Gilac Décor has decked it with flowers for you!' 'A revolution in refrigeration – complete with brand-new freezer compartment and butter softener!' 'An electric razor on the cutting edge of progress – hexagonal, antimagnetic!'

These are what David Riesman calls marginal differences; perhaps it would be more exact to call them inessential differences. The fact is that at the level of the industrial object and its technological coherence the demand for personalization can be met only in inessentials. The sole way to personalize cars is for the manufacturer to take a serially produced chassis, a serially pro-duced engine, then change a few external characteristics or add a couple of accessory features. A car cannot be personalized in its essence as a technical object, but only in its inessential aspects.

6. I shall come back to this system later.

Of course, the more the object must respond to the demands of personalization, the more its essential characteristics are burdened by extrinsic requirements. Coachwork is weighed down by accessories, for example, even to the point where technical norms for a vehicle such as fluidity of line and mobility are contravened. 'Marginal' difference is thus not solely marginal, for it can run counter to an object's technical essence. The personalization function is not just an added value – it is also a parasitic value. Indeed, from the technological standpoint it is impossible to conceive of an object in an industrial system being personalized without thereby losing some measure of its optimal technical quality. The dictates of production bear the most responsibility here, for they play unrestrainedly on inessentials in order to promote consumption.

So, when you choose YOUR Ariane, you have forty-two colour combinations to select from (including solid colours and two-colour versions). De luxe hub-caps are available from your dealer when you buy your car. The point is, of course, that all these 'specific' differences are themselves picked up and mass-produced in serial form. *And this secondary seriality is what constitutes fashion.* Ultimately, therefore, every object is a model, yet at the same time there are no more models. What we are left with in the end are successive limited series, a disjointed transition to ever more restricted series based on ever more minute and ever more specific differences. There are simply no more absolute models – and no more serial objects devoid of value categorically opposed to them. If it were otherwise, there would be no psychological basis for choice – and hence no cultural system. Or at least, no cultural system capable of embracing modern industrial society in its entirety.

The Ideal Nature of Models

How does this system of personalization and integration work? Its operation depends in the first place on the fact that each 'specific' difference continually negates and disavows the object's serial reality to the benefit of the model. Objectively, as we have seen, such differences are inessential. Furthermore, they often mask technical shortcomings.[7] They are in fact differences by default. They are always experienced, however, as features conferring distinction, indicative of value – as differences of overmeasure. It is thus not necessary for a concrete model to exist for every category of objects, and in many cases none does: minuscule differences, invariably apprehended as positive, quite suffice to extend the series, to create the aspiration towards a model that may be merely virtual. Such marginal differences are the motor of the series, and fuel the mechanism of integration.

Series and model should not be conceived of as two poles of a formal opposition, with the model being viewed as a sort of essence which – once divided and multiplied, so to speak, by virtue of the concept of 'mass' – gives birth to the series. From this standpoint, the model appears as a more concrete or denser state of the object which enables it to be retailed or disseminated as a series formed in its own image. The model/series distinction is often used in this way to evoke a kind of entropy homologous to the degeneration of higher forms of energy into heat. This conception, which deduces the series from the model, is completely at loggerheads with lived experience, which implies a continual inductive movement *from* the series *into* the model – less a degenerative (and literally unlivable) process than a siphoning process.

The fact is that the model is everywhere discernible in the series. It inhabits the slightest 'specific' difference between one object and the next. Above we noted the same tendency in collecting, where each item in a collection is marked by a relative difference which momentarily lends it a privileged status – the status, in effect, of a model; all such relative differences refer to all the others, and in aggregate they constitute absolute difference – or rather, funda-

7. The technical downgrading of serial objects will be discussed in a moment; see also the section on 'Gadgets and Robots' above.

mentally, just the *idea of absolute difference*, which is precisely what the Model is. We may say of a model that it exists or that it does not exist. The Facel-Vega certainly exists, yet all the variations in colour or capacity refer ultimately only to the *idea* of the Facel-Vega. Indeed, *it is essential that the model be no more than the idea of the model*. Only on this condition can it be present in every single relative difference, and thus integrate the whole series. If the Facel-Vega actually existed, the 'personalized' satisfaction to be derived from any other car would be radically compromised. On the other hand, the idealizing assumption that it exists serves as a justification and solid underpinning for personalization *vis-à-vis* something that is precisely *not* the Facel-Vega. The model is neither impoverished nor high-wrought: it is a generic image manufactured through the imaginary assumption of all relative differences. Its fascination stems directly from the tendency that causes the series to negate itself from one difference to the next; it is the fascination of intense movement, proliferating reference, never-ending substitution – in short, a formal idealization of transcendence. What is integrated and invested in the model is the whole evolution of the series.

The fact that the model is just an idea is, moreover, the only thing that makes the actual process of personalization possible. The notion that consciousness could be personalized in an object is absurd: it is personalized, rather, in a difference, because only a difference, by referring to the absolute singularity of the Model, can thereby refer at the same time to what is really being signified here, namely the absolute singularity of the user, the buyer or (as we saw above) the collector. Paradoxically, then, it is through an idea that is both vague and shared by all that everyone may come to experience himself as unique. Reciprocally, it is only continual self-individualization on the basis of the range of serial distinctions that allows the imaginary consensus of the idea of the model to be revived. Personalization and integration go strictly hand in hand. That is the *miracle of the system*.

From the Model to the Series

The Technical Deficit of the Serial Object
Now that we have analysed the formal play of differences by means
of which the serial object manifests itself, and is experienced, as
model, it is time to examine the *real* differences that distinguish
the model from the series. For naturally the upward tendency of
differential valorization relative to the *ideal model* masks the
inverse reality of the destructuring and drastic downgrading of
the serial object relative to the *real model.*

Of all the servitudes visited upon the serial object, the most
obvious concerns its durability and its technical quality. The
imperatives of personalization and production combined cause
a proliferation of accessory features to the detriment of strict use
value. The first effect of all the innovations and all the vagaries of
fashion is to render objects more shoddy and ephemeral. Vance
Packard points up this tendency, listing 'three different ways that
products can be made obsolescent':

> *Obsolescence of function.* In this situation an existing product
> becomes outmoded when a product is introduced that performs
> the function better.
>
> *Obsolescence of quality.* Here, when it is planned, a product
> breaks down or wears out at a given time, usually not too
> distant.
>
> *Obsolescence of desirability.* In this situation a product that is still
> sound in terms of quality or performance becomes 'worn out' in
> our minds because a styling or other change makes it seem less
> desirable.
>
> The first type of obsolescence – the functional type – is
> certainly laudable . . .[8]

8. Vance Packard, *The Waste Makers* (New York: David McKay, 1960), p. 55.

The last two aspects of this scheme work together. The accelerated replacement of models itself affects the object's quality. Thus stockings may now come in all colours, but their quality will have declined (or perhaps research and development will have been cut back to finance an advertising campaign). Should the manipulated fluctuations of fashion fail to restimulate demand, recourse can be had to an artificial sub-functionality – to 'deliberately shoddy construction'. Packard quotes an industrial designer, Brooks Stevens, to the effect that 'Our whole economy is based on planned obsolescence, and everybody who can read without moving his lips should know it.'[9] And he finds that Oliver Wendell Holmes was prophetically close to the mark 'when he wrote of that wonderful one-hoss shay which was built in such a logical way that on a given day "it went to pieces all at once" '.[10] Thus certain American car parts are designed not to survive more than sixty thousand kilometres of driving. As manufacturers themselves will discreetly admit, the quality of most serial objects could be substantially improved with no significant increase in production costs. Deliberately debased parts are just as expensive to manufacture as normal ones . . . BUT THE OBJECT CANNOT BE ALLOWED TO ESCAPE FROM EPHEMERALITY OR FROM FASHION. This is the fundamental characteristic of the series: the objects that compose it are weakened on a systematic basis. In a world of (relative) affluence, *the shoddiness of objects replaces the scarcity of objects as the expression of poverty.* The series is forcefully imposed for a brief cross-section of time; its universe is distinctly perishable. THE OBJECT CANNOT BE ALLOWED TO ESCAPE DEATH. Unfettered technological progress would doubtless override this mortality of the object, but the strategy of production strives constantly to maintain it.[11] Ernest Dichter speaks, in connection with selling, of

9. Ibid., p. 54.
10. Ibid., p. 57.
11. Of course this tendency is liable to be slowed by the operation of competition. But in countries (such as the United States) where mono-polistic production is the norm, true competition has long been nonexistent.

a 'strategy of desire'; we might well speak here of a strategy of frustration. These two strategies together serve to ensure the exclusive rule of the goals of production – indeed, production has now emerged as an all-surpassing agency with the power not merely of life but also of death over objects.[12]

The model, by contrast, is privileged in that it lasts (though only in a relative sense, for it too is caught in the speeded-up cycle of objects). It is granted solidity, entitled to 'loyalty'. Paradoxically, it has come to dominate an area traditionally reserved, it would seem, for the series, namely use value. This superiority of the model, reinforced by the influence of fashion – that is, the combination of technical and formal qualities – are what constitute its superior 'functionality'.

The 'Style' Deficit of the Serial Object
In parallel fashion, when we compare the serial object to the model we find that the serial object's physical attributes, just like its technical ones, are distinctly inferior. Consider the material used, for example: the steel and leather armchair on show at Airborne will crop up in aluminium and leatherette at Dubonbois Home Furnishings. The glass partition of a model interior will have a plastic echo in the serial version. Solid wood furniture will reappear in a whitewood veneer. A fine woollen or wild-silk dress will proliferate in ready-to-wear form in a wool mixture or in rayon. It is the heft, hardiness, grain or 'warmth' of a material whose presence or absence serves as a marker of difference. Such tactile characteristics are close to the most profound defining qualities of the model – far more so than the visual values of colour and form, which are more easily transposed to series

12. It must nonetheless be acknowledged that this cynical strategic perspective is not the only villain here, for there is unquestionably a degree of willing compliance on the part of consumers. Many people would be disconcerted indeed at the prospect of having to keep the same car for twenty or thirty years, even if it continued to meet all their needs. On this point, see 'Gadgets and Robots' above.

because they are better suited to the needs of marginal differentiation.

Of course, even colours and forms are never integrated unscathed into a series. Finish is wanting, as is inventiveness. Faithfully transposed as they may be, forms suffer a subtle loss of their originality. What the serial object lacks is thus less the material itself than a certain consistency between material and form which ensures the model's finished quality. In series this consistency, this set of necessary relations, is destroyed for the sake of the differentiating action of forms, colours and accessories. Style gives way to combination. The process of downgrading referred to above in connection with the technical aspect is here more of a destructuring tendency. In the case of the model object, details and the workings of details are not the point. Rolls-Royces are black, and that's that.[13] The model is literally *hors série*, without peer – hence out of the game: only the 'personalization' of objects allows the play of differences to expand in proportion with the length of the series (as when fifteen or twenty different shades are available for a single make of car); at the other extreme – the return to pure utility – the play of differences once more ceases to exist (for a very long time the Citroën 2CV came only in a grey that was hardly a colour at all). The model has a harmony, a unity, a homogeneity, a consistency of space, form, substance, and function; it is, in short, a syntax. The serial object is merely juxtaposition, haphazard combination, inarticulate discourse. As a detotalized form, it is nothing more than a collection of details relating in mechanical fashion to parallel series. Suppose that the uniqueness of the aforementioned armchair lies in its particular combination of tawny leather, black steel, general silhouette and mobilization of space. The corresponding serial object will emerge with plasticized leather, no tawniness, the metal lighter or galvanized, the overall configuration altered and the relationship to

13. Or sometimes grey, it is true. But the 'moral' paradigm remains in place (see above, p. 31).

space diminished. The object as a whole is thus destructured: its substance is assigned to the series of objects in imitation leather, its tawniness is now a brown common to thousands of other objects, its legs are indistinguishable from those of any tubular chair, and so on. The object is no longer anything more than a conglomeration of details and the crossroads of a variety of series. Here is another example: a luxury car is in a red described as 'unique'. What 'unique' implies here is not simply that this red can be found nowhere else, but also that it is one with the car's other attributes: the red is not an 'extra'. But no sooner does this colour appear ever so slightly changed on a more 'commercial' car than it becomes the red of thousands of others – a mere detail or accessory feature of cars that are red as an 'extra', because they might just as well be green or black.

Class Differences

By now the reader should be getting a better feel for the distinction between model and series. More even than its consistency, it is the nuancing of the model that makes it distinctive. At present we are witnessing an attempt to stylize serial interiors – to 'bring good taste to the masses'. The result, generally speaking, is 'all in the same colour' and 'all in the same style': one may have a 'baroque living-room', a 'kitchen in blue', etc. What is presented as a 'style', however, is fundamentally a mere stereotype, the unnuanced generalization of a particular detail or aspect. The fact is that *the nuance (within a unity)* has come to characterize the model, while *difference (within uniformity)* has come to characterize the series. Nuances in this sense are infinite in number, being emphases ever susceptible of reinvention in accordance with an open-ended syntax. Differences are finite in number, being the result of systematic variations on a single paradigm. Let us not be misled by the apparent scarcity of nuances and the apparent profusion of differences (due to their massive dissemination), for structurally speaking the fact remains that nuances are inexhaustible (the model in this connection may be said to come close to the work of art), whereas the serial difference is part of a finite combinatorial system or tablature which, though it no doubt changes continually in response to fashion, is nevertheless, for each synchronic moment considered, limited by and strictly subject to the dictates of production. In sum, the series offers the immense majority of people a restricted range of choices, while a tiny minority enjoy access to the model and its infinite nuances. For the majority a range which, however extensive it may be, is composed of invariable elements – generally the most obvious ones; for the minority a multitude of random possibilities. For the majority a set code of values; for the minority endless invention. We are thus indeed clearly dealing with class status and class distinctions.

The redundancy of its secondary features is an attempt to compensate for the serial object's loss of essential qualities. Colours, contrasts and the 'modern' look are thus overloaded with significance; indeed, the serial object's modernity is stressed at the precise moment when the model is sloughing modernity off. Whereas the model retains an airiness, a discretion, and a 'naturalness' that is the epitome of culture, the serial object remains stuck fast in its quest for uniqueness, and betrays a constrained culture, an optimism in the worst of taste, and an empty-headed humanism. For the serial object has its own class-specific script, its own rhetoric – just as the model has *its* own rhetoric of reticence, veiled functionality, perfection and eclecticism.[14]

Another expression of this redundancy is accumulation. There are always too many objects in serial interiors. And too many objects means too little space. Promiscuity or saturation occur as

14. In a system of this kind the two opposing terms cannot help but carry a surplus of meaning, for each is defined by reference to the other, and is to that extent redundant. Moreover, this redundancy of surplus meaning is the thing which, from the psycho-sociological point of view, defines the mode in which the system is directly experienced; although the present account may occasionally suggest the contrary, this can never be a system of pure structural oppositions.

reactions to scarcity. Loss of quality must be made up for by the sheer number of objects.[15] The model has its own space, in which objects are neither too close to one another nor too far apart. The model interior is given structure by these relative distances, and if anything it tends towards the opposite kind of redundancy: connotation by emptiness.[16]

The Present as Privilege
Another axis of comparison in distinguishing model from series is time. We have noted that the serial object is designed not to last. Just like generations of people in underdeveloped societies, generations of objects in consumer society are short-lived, and one very soon gives way to the next. Where the abundance of objects increases, it always does so under the constraints of a calculated scarcity. That, however, is the problem of the object's technical durability. The immediate experience of the object, as determined by fashion, is another matter.

A rapid sociological examination of the market in antiques reveals that it is governed by the same laws and organized fundamentally in accordance with the same model/series scheme as the market in 'industrial' products. It emerges that within the potpourri which, in the case of furniture, includes everything from baroque to Chippendale, from Medici writing-tables to Art Nouveau and fake rustic, it is always possible (given the necessary financial resources and culture) to go higher and higher up the ladder of 'established' values in search of the focus of one's 'personal' mooring back in history. There is a status attached to regression in time, and one's means are liable to determine whether one acquires a genuine ancient Greek vase or a mere

15. The bourgeois tradition inclined naturally towards redundancy and accumulation (bourgeois houses were often stuffed to the rafters). The more 'functional' approach of modern interior design runs counter to that tendency, however, so that the over-occupation of space in a modern house is more seriously inconsistent than in a traditional one.
16. See the discussion of 'formal connotation' above, pp. 59 ff.

reproduction, a Roman amphora or a Spanish pitcher. In the world of objects the past and the exotic have a social dimension, a relationship to culture and income. The leisured classes go to their antique dealers for medieval, *haute époque* or French Regency furniture; the cultivated middle classes scour flea-market junk stalls for the wherewithal to re-create a solidly bourgeois cultural décor with 'authentic' peasant touches; and rustic themes are just perfect for service-sector employees enamoured of the largely bourgeoisified country interiors of the previous generation, or of provincial 'period styles' that are really hybrid forms impossible to date and having nothing but the vaguest echo of a 'period'. Each social class thus has its very own cut-price museum. Only workers and peasants still largely shun antiques. True, they have neither the leisure nor the money required, but the chief reason is that they are not as yet touched by the acculturation phenomenon affecting other classes. (Not that they consciously refuse it – rather, they simply fall outside its sphere of influence.) Nor, however, do they care for the modern and the 'experimental', for new 'creations' or for anything 'avant-garde'. Their own museum is often limited to cheap hardware and a folk-loric world of china or earthenware animals, gewgaws, decorated mugs, framed mementoes, and the like – a whole stereotyped iconography quite liable to be found cheek by jowl with the very last word in electrical household appliances. This is in no way to downplay the need to 'personalize' – which is the same for all; it is just that the only people who can regress in time are those who can afford it. Difference – in this case culturalized difference – is what creates value, and it has to be paid for. Models and series are just as easy to find in the realm of cultural nostalgia as in the immediacy of fashion.

If we look to see what in this range of possibilities has the maximum value, we find that it is either the most avant-garde of objects or objects from the past with an aristocratic dimension: either a glass-and-aluminium villa with elliptical contours or an eighteenth-century château – either the ideal future or the *ancien régime*. Conversely the pure series, the unmarked term, is located, not exactly in the present, which is, along with the future, the time of the avant-garde and of the model, nor in that transcendent past which is the preserve of the well-to-do and their acquired culture, but instead in an 'immediate' past, an indefinite past which is fundamentally a sort of belated present, a limbo into which yesterday's models have just recently fallen. In clothing styles the pace of change is very rapid, and the office workers of today wear dresses derived from last season's *haute couture* models. In furnishing, however, what has wide currency in the present is whatever was in high fashion a few years or even a generation ago. Serial time here is always the time of the wave before, so to speak. As far as their furniture is concerned, most people live in a time which is not theirs, a time of generality, of insignificance, the time of that which is not modern but not yet antique (and, no doubt, never will be antique): the equivalent in time of suburban impersonality in space. By comparison with the model the series does not stand merely for a loss of uniqueness of style, of nuances, and of authenticity: it stands also for the loss of the real dimension of time – for it belongs to a kind of empty sector of everyday life, a negative realm automatically filled up with senescent models. For only models change; series merely follow upon one another in the wake of a model with which they can never catch up. That is where their true unreality lies.

A Misadventure of the Person

'The product now in demand is neither a staple nor a machine, it is a personality,' according to David Riesman.[17] Personal achievement is indeed an *obligation* haunting the modern consumer in the context of the forced mobility imposed by the model/series system (which is, incidentally, but one aspect of a much larger structure of social mobility and aspiration). In the

17. David Riesman, in collaboration with Reuel Denny and Nathan Glazer, *The Lonely Crowd: A Study of the Changing American Character* (New Haven: Yale University Press/London: Geoffrey Cumberlege, Oxford University Press, 1950), p. 46.

area which concerns us here, this constraint is paradoxical: it is clear that in the act of personalized consumption the subject, in his very insistence on being a *subject*, succeeds in manifesting himself only as an *object* of economic demand. His project, filtered and fragmented in advance, is dashed by the very process that is supposed to realize it. Since 'specific differences' are produced on an industrial scale, any choice he can make is ossified from the outset; only the *illusion* of personal distinctiveness remains. In seeking to add that 'something' which will make for uniqueness, consciousness is reified in an even more intimate way, precisely because it is reified right down to that particular detail. Such is the paradox of alienation: a living choice is embodied in dead differences, indulgence in which dooms the subjective project to self-negation and despair.

This is the ideological function of the system: increasing status is nothing but a game, for all differences are integrated in advance. The very deceit with which the whole arrangement is shot through is an integral part of that arrangement, on account of the system's perpetual forward flight.

Yet are we quite justified in speaking of alienation here? Overall, the system of manipulated personalization is experienced by the vast majority of consumers as freedom. Only to a critical eye does this freedom appear merely formal, and the process of personalization as a misadventure of the person. Even in cases where advertising motivates on the basis of nothing at all (as where the same product goes by different brand names, where differences are illusory or where quality is erratic) – even where the choice is undoubtedly a trap – it still cannot be denied that even superficial differences are real as soon as someone invests them with value. How can we contest the satisfaction of a person who buys a dustbin decorated with flowers or an 'antimagnetic' razor? No theory of needs can authorize us to assign priority to one actually experienced satisfaction over any other. If the demand for self-worth is so deep-seated that in the absence of any alternative it embodies itself in a 'personalized' object, what basis do we have for rejecting this tendency, and in the name of what 'authentic' essential value could we do so?

The Ideology of Models

The system we have been describing reposes upon an ideology of democracy; it claims to be an aspect of social progress – to be what makes it possible for all gradually to gain access to models by virtue of a continual sociological upward movement which is carrying each stratum of society in turn to greater material luxury, and, from one 'personalized' difference to the next, ever closer to the absolute model.

Two objections may be raised to this account of things. In the first place, we find that we are in fact, in our 'consumer society', farther and farther away from equality before the object. The idea of the model has been obliged to seek refuge, concretely, in ever more subtle and definitive differences: such and such a skirt length, such and such a shade of red, such and such an advance in stereophony, or the few weeks that separate *haute couture* from mass distribution courtesy of Prisunic. All extremely ephemeral things – yet all very expensive indeed. A seeming equality attaches to the fact that all objects obey the same 'functional' imperative. But, as we have seen, this formal democratization of cultural status conceals other inequalities which are far more serious in that they affect the very reality of the object, its technical quality, its substance and its life-span. The privileges of the model are no longer institutional, it is true; they have, as it were, been internalized – but this has merely made them more tenacious. Just as, in the wake of the bourgeois revolution, no other classes ever gradually acquired positions of political responsibility, so likewise, in the wake of the industrial revolution, consumers have never won equality before the object.

The second point is that it is a delusion to take the model for an ideal point which the series will eventually be able to rejoin. The possession of objects frees us only as possessors, and always refers us back to the infinite freedom to possess more objects: the only progression possible here is up the ladder of objects, but this is a ladder that leads nowhere, being itself responsible for nourishing the inaccessible abstraction of the model. For the model is basically merely an idea, that is, a *transcendence internal to the system* – and the system in its entirety can continue in its forward flight indefinitely. There is no prospect of a model entering a series without being simultaneously replaced by another model. The whole system proceeds *en bloc*, but models replace one another without ever being transcended as such and without successive series, for their part, ever achieving self-transcendence as series. Models move along faster than series: they inhabit the present, whereas series float somewhere between past and present, wearing themselves out in the vain attempt to catch up with models. This perpetual cycle of aspiration and disillusion, dynamically orchestrated at the level of production, constitutes the arena in which objects are pursued.

There is a kind of inevitability at work here. Once a whole society articulates itself around models and focuses on them; once production strives in every way possible towards the systematic breaking down of models into series, and series in their turn into marginal differences or combinative variants, until at last objects come to have a status just as ephemeral as that of words or images; once the systematic stretching of series turns the whole edifice into a paradigm, but a paradigm whose ordering is irreversible, in that the ladder of status is fixed and the rules of the game of status are the same for everyone; once we fall under the sway of this managed convergence, this planned flimsiness, this continually eroded synchrony – then all negation becomes impossible. There are no more overt contradictions, no more structural changes, no more social dialectics. For the tendency which seems, in accordance with technical progress, to mobilize the whole system in no way challenges that system's ability to remain unmoving and stable in itself. Everything is in movement, everything shifts before our eyes, everything is continually being transformed – yet nothing really changes. This is a society whose embrace of technological progress enables it to make every conceivable revolution, just so long as those revolutions are confined within its bounds. For all its increased productivity, our society does not open the door to one single *structural* change.

II Credit

Rights and Duties of the Consumer-Citizen

Today, then, objects appear under the sign of differentiation and choice – but they also appear (or at least, all key objects do) under the sign of *credit*. When you buy something you certainly have to pay for it, but the *choice* is yours 'free', and by the same token credit terms are proposed as a free gift, as a kind of bonus from the world of production. The unstated assumption is that credit is the consumer's right, and ultimately an economic right of the citizen. Restriction of any kind on the possibility of buying on credit is felt to be a retaliatory measure on the part of the State; to do away with such arrangements – which is in any case unthinkable – would be experienced by society at large as the abolition of a freedom. For advertising, credit is a decisive argument in the 'strategy of desire', and its role is comparable in every way to any other quality of the object on offer; it is on a par in customer motivation with choice, 'personalization' and the rhetoric of promotion, of which last it is the tactical complement. The way in which the model is anticipated in the series is paralleled in the case of credit by the enjoyment of objects ahead of time; the psychological context is the same.

In principle the credit system does not affect the serial object more or less than it affects the model, and there is nothing to stop anyone buying a Jaguar on hire purchase. In actuality, however, custom decrees that the de luxe model be paid for cash down; things bought on credit tend simply not to be models. There is a logic of status according to which the prestige of a cash purchase is one of the privileges of the model, while the constraint of periodic payments contributes to the psychological shortfall associated with the serial object.

A certain puritanism has long sensed some moral danger in credit, and placed on-the-spot payment among the bourgeois virtues. It must be admitted, however, that psychological resistance of this kind is gradually diminishing. Where it persists, it is merely a relic of a traditional notion of property, and largely confined to the class of small owners still faithful to the notions of inheritance, thrift and the family future. These survivals are sure to die out in time. Once property had priority over use; now the reverse is true, and the extension of credit, among other phenomena defined by David Riesman, marks the gradual transition from an 'acquisitive' civilization to a practical one. Credit customers are gradually learning how to make use of objects in complete freedom as though they were already 'theirs'. The difference, of course, is that while such objects are being paid for they are simultaneously wearing out: the final payment-due date is not unrelated to the 'replacement-due' date – indeed, as we know, some American firms strive to make the two intervening periods coincide exactly. There is always the risk, therefore, as in the event of defectiveness or loss, that an object will be, so to speak, used up before it is paid up. Even when credit seems to have been perfectly integrated into everyday life, this danger is the basis of an insecurity that was never experienced in connection with the 'patrimonial' object. Such an object was mine: I owed nothing. An object bought on credit will be mine when I have paid for it: it is conjugated, as it were, in the future perfect.

The anxiety that attaches to periodic payments is very specific. It eventually sets in train a parallel process which weighs down on us day after day even though we never become conscious of the objective relationship involved. It haunts the human project, not immediate practice. An object that is mortgaged escapes us in time, and has in fact escaped us from the outset. It flees us, and its flight echoes that of the serial object ever vainly striving towards the model. This dual movement of things away from our grasp is what creates the latent fragility and ever-imminent disappointments of the world of objects that surrounds us.

In the end the credit system merely exemplifies what is a very general way of relating to objects in the modern context. Indeed, it is quite possible to live on credit without sitting amid a year's worth of credit invoices for car, fridge and television, because the model/series mechanism, with its obligatory orientation towards the model, is a handicap in its own right. This mechanism governs the realm of social advancement, which consequently becomes a realm of handicapped aspiration. *We are forever behindhand relative to our objects.* They are here before us, yet they are already a year away, located either in that final payment or else in the next model by which they are bound to be replaced. So credit simply transfers a basic psychological situation onto the economic plane; the obligation to follow a sequence is the same at both levels, whether it is economic, as with successive hire-purchase payments, or psycho-sociological, as in the systematic and ever-accelerating succession of series and models. In any event, we experience our objects in a predefined, mortgaged temporal mode. If there are now barely any restrictions on the use of credit, perhaps the reason is that *all* our objects today are apprehended as if they were obtained on credit, as debts incurred to society as a whole – debts that are always susceptible of adjustment, always fluctuating, always prey to chronic inflation and devaluation. Much in the same way as our earlier discussion of 'personalization' led us to conclude that this was far more than an advertising gimmick, that it was in fact a key ideological notion, so likewise credit must be viewed as far more than a financial arrangement, for it is nothing less than a fundamental dimension of our society and in effect a new ethical system.

The Precedence of Consumption: A New Ethic

A single generation has witnessed the eclipse of the notions of patrimony and of fixed capital. Until our parents' generation, objects once acquired were owned in the full sense, for they were the material expression of work done. It is still not very long since buying a dining-table and chairs, or a car, represented the end-point of a sustained exercise of thrift. People worked dreaming of what they might later acquire; life was lived in accordance with the puritan notion of effort and its reward – and objects finally won represented repayment for the past and security for the future. They were, in short, a capital. Today objects are with us before they are earned, they steal a march on the sum total of effort, of labour, that they embody, so that in a sense *their consumption precedes their production.* True, these objects, which I merely make use of, no longer impose any patrimonial responsibility on me; they are bequeathed to me by nobody and I, in turn, shall bequeath them to nobody. They do, however, exert another kind of constraint, for they hang over me as debts as yet unsettled. If they no longer locate me in a relationship to a family or customary group, I am nevertheless brought into relation through them with society at large and its agencies (the economic and financial order, the fluctuations of fashion, and so forth). And I must pay for them over and over again, month by month, or replace them every year. This means that everything has changed: the significance these objects have for me, the projects they embody, their objective future, and mine. It is worth pondering the fact that for centuries generations of people succeeded one another in an unchanging décor of objects which were longer-lived than they, whereas now many generations of objects will follow upon one another at an ever-accelerating pace during a single human lifetime. Where once man imposed his rhythm upon objects, now objects impose their disjointed rhythm – their unpredictable and sudden manner of being present, of breaking down or replacing one another without ever aging – upon human beings. Thus the status of a whole civilization changes along with the way in which its everyday objects make themselves present and the way in which they are enjoyed. In a patriarchal domestic economy founded on inheritance and stable rents, consumption could never conceivably precede production. In accordance with good Cartesian and moral logic, work preceded its fruit as cause precedes effect. That ascetic mode of accumulation, rooted in forethought, in sacrifice, and in a resorption of needs that created great tension within the individual, was the foundation of a whole civilization of thrift which enjoyed its own heroic period before expiring in the anachronistic figure of the *rentier* – indeed, of the ruined *rentier*, who in this century has perforce learnt the historical lesson of the vanity of traditional morality and traditional economic calculation. By dint of living within their means, whole generations have ended up living far below their means. Work, merit, accumulation – all the virtues of an era whose pinnacle was the concept of property are still discernible in the objects that stand as witness to that time, objects whose lost generations continue to haunt the petty-bourgeois interior.

The Obligation to Buy

Today a new morality has been born. Precedence of consumption over accumulation, forward flight, forced investment, speeded-up consumption, chronic inflation (implying the absurdity of saving) – these are the motors of our whole present system of buying first and paying off later in labour. Credit has thus brought us back to a situation that is in fact feudal in character, reminiscent as it is of the arrangement under which a portion of labour would be allocated in advance, as serf labour, to the feudal lord. There is a difference, however, for our system, unlike feudalism, reposes on complicity: modern consumers spontaneously embrace and accept the unending constraint that is imposed on them. They buy so that society can continue to produce, this so that they can continue to work, and this in turn so that they can pay for what they have bought. Witness the following American advertising slogans, noted by Vance Packard, which make the point very well: 'Buy days mean pay days – and pay days mean better days!'; 'Buy now – the job you save may be your own!'; 'Buy your way to prosperity!'[18]

The illusionism is truly remarkable: society appears to extend credit to you in exchange for a formal freedom, but in reality it is you who are giving credit to society, alienating your future in the process. Of course the system of production still depends fundamentally on the exploitation of labour-power, but today it is strongly reinforced by the circular consensus or collusion whereby subjection itself is experienced as freedom, and is thus transformed into an independent and durable system. In every individual the consumer colludes with the production system while having no relationship to the producer – the victim of the system – that he also is. Paradoxically, this split between producer and consumer is the mainstay of social integration, because everything is done so that it can never take the living and critical form of a contradiction.

The Miracle of Buying

The advantage of credit (as of advertising) is indeed the dual dimension it bestows upon buying and its objective determinants. Buying on credit amounts to the total appropriation of an object for a fraction of its real value. A minimal investment for a profit out of all proportion to it. Payments are relegated to a dimly perceived future, and the object is acquired in exchange for a symbolic gesture. This transaction mirrors the behaviour of the mythomaniac, who for the price of a made-up story receives a quite disproportionate measure of attention from his audience.

18. *The Waste Makers*, p. 17.

His real investment is minimal, while the benefits are extraordinary, for he acquires all the virtues of reality on the strength, practically speaking, of a mere sign. He too lives on credit – in the shape of the credulousness of other people. Now this inversion of the normal way of transforming reality – which proceeds from work to the product of work, and founds the traditional temporality of the logic of knowledge as of everyday praxis – this premature reaping of benefits is nothing less than *magical*. Likewise, what the buyer consumes and appropriates thanks to credit, along with the object prematurely acquired, is the myth of magical functionality promoted by the only society capable of offering him such possibilities of immediate self-realization. Naturally, he will very soon come face to face with socio-economic reality, just as the mythomaniac must sooner or later confront the spuriousness of his claims. Once unmasked, the mythomaniac either collapses or takes refuge in another tall tale. The buyer on the never-never is similarly liable to run up against unmeetable payment-due dates, and there is a good chance that he will seek psychological reassurance in this situation by buying some other item on credit. Forward flight is usual with this kind of behaviour, and the marvellous thing is that no causal connection is ever made, either by the mythomaniac between the story he tells and the failure he eventually experiences (for he learns nothing from this cold dash of reality), or by the buyer on credit between the gratification he obtains magically from his purchase and the payments he must subsequently meet. In this respect the credit system is the acme of man's irresponsibility towards himself: the buyer alienates the payer, and even though they are in fact the same person, the system ensures, by separating them in time, that they never become aware of the fact.

The Ambiguity of the Domestic Object

In sum, credit pretends to promote a civilization of modern consumers at last freed from the constraints of property, but in reality it institutes a whole system of integration which combines social mythology with brutal economic pressure. Credit is an ethic, but it is also a politics. The tactic of credit works in tandem with that of personalization to give objects a socio-political function they never used to have. We no longer live in the age of serfdom or in the age of usury, but both these constraints have been incorporated in abstract and amplified form into the realm of credit. Credit is a social realm, a temporal realm, a realm of things by virtue of which, and by virtue of the strategy that imposes it, objects are able to fulfil their function as accelerators and multipliers of tasks, satisfactions and expenditures. They thus become a kind of trampoline, their very inertia serving as a centrifugal force which lends everyday life its rhythm – its tendency to forward flight, its precariousness and disequilibrium.

At the same time, objects, on which domesticity once depended as a means of escape from the pressures of society, now on the contrary serve to shackle the domestic universe to the circuits and constraints of the social one. By means of credit – which is a free gift and a formal freedom but also a social sanction, a form of subjection and a fatality at the very heart of things – domesticity is directly colonized: it acquires a kind of social dimension, but in the very worst sense. The most extreme and absurd effects of credit are eloquent: for example, when car payments are so pressing that the buyer cannot afford petrol for his vehicle, we have reached the point where the human project, filtered and fragmented by economic pressures, begins to feed upon itself. A fundamental truth about the present system emerges here too: *objects now are by no means meant to be owned and used but solely to be produced and bought.* In other words, they are structured as a function neither of needs nor of a more rational organization of the world, but instead constitute a system determined entirely by an ideological regime of production and social integration. Indeed, private objects properly so called no longer exist: thanks to their multiple use, it is the social order of production, with its own particular complicities, which now haunts the intimate world of the consumer and his consciousness. This penetration also marks the fading of any prospect of effectively contesting or transcending that social order.

III *Advertising*

Discourse on Objects and Discourse-As-Object

Any analysis of the system *of* objects must ultimately imply an analysis of discourse *about* objects – that is to say, an analysis of promotional 'messages' (comprising image and discourse). For advertising is not simply an adjunct to the system of objects; it cannot be detached therefrom, nor can it be restricted to its 'proper' function (there is no such thing as advertising strictly confined to the supplying of information). Indeed, advertising is now an irremovable aspect of the system of objects precisely by virtue of its disproportionateness. This lack of proportion is the 'functional' apotheosis of the system. Advertising in its entirety constitutes a useless and unnecessary universe. It is pure connotation. It contributes nothing to production or to the direct practical application of things, yet it plays an integral part in the system of objects, not merely because it relates to consumption but also because it itself becomes an object to be consumed. A clear distinction must be drawn in connection with advertising's dual status as a discourse on the object and as an object in its own right. It is as a useless, unnecessary discourse that it comes to be consumable as a cultural object. What achieves autonomy and fulfilment through advertising is thus the whole system that I have been describing at the level of objects: the entire apparatus of personalization and imposed differentiation; of proliferation of the inessential and subordination of technical requirements to the requirements of production and consumption; of dysfunctionality and secondary functionality. Since its function is almost entirely secondary, and since both image and discourse play largely allegorical roles in it, advertising supplies us with the ideal object and casts a particularly revealing light upon the system of objects. And since, like all heavily connoted systems, it is self-referential,[19] we may safely rely on advertising to tell us what it is that we consume *through* objects.

Advertising in the Indicative and in the Imperative

Advertising sets itself the task of supplying information about particular products and promoting their sale. In principle this 'objective' function is still its fundamental purpose.[20] The supplying of information has nevertheless given way to persuasion – even to what Vance Packard calls 'hidden persuasion', the aim of which is a completely managed consumption. The supposed threat this poses of a totalitarian conditioning of man and his needs has provoked great alarm. Studies have shown, however, that advertising's pervasive power is not as great as had been supposed. A saturation point is in fact soon reached: competing messages tend to cancel each other out, and many claims fail to convince on account of their sheer excessiveness. Moreover, injunctions and exhortations give rise to all kinds of counter-motivations and resistances, whether rational or irrational, among them the refusal of passivity, the desire not to be 'taken over', negative reactions to hyperbole, to repetition, and so on. In short, the discourse of advertising is just as likely to dissuade as to persuade, and consumers, though not entirely immune, appear to exercise a good deal of discretion when it comes to the advertising message.

19. See Roland Barthes's account of the system of fashion: *Système de la mode* (Paris: Seuil, 1967).
20. We should not forget, however, that the earliest advertisements were for miracle cures, home remedies, and the like; they supplied information, therefore, but information only of the most tendentious kind.

Having said this, let us not be misled by the *avowed* aim of that message; while advertising may well fail to sell the consumer on a particular brand – Omo, Simca or Frigidaire – it does sell him on something else, something much more fundamental to the global social order than Omo or Frigidaire – something, indeed, for which such brand names are merely a cover.

Just as the object's function may ultimately amount merely to the provision of a justification for the latent meanings that the object imposes, so in advertising (and all the more so inasmuch as it is the more purely connotative system) the product designated – that is, its denotation or description – tends to be merely an effective mask concealing a confused process of integration.

So even though we may be getting better and better at resisting advertising in the *imperative*, we are at the same time becoming ever more susceptible to advertising in the *indicative* – that is, to its actual *existence* as a product to be consumed at a secondary level, and as the clear *expression* of a culture. It is in this sense that we do indeed 'believe' in advertising: what we consume in this way is the luxury of a society that projects itself as an agency for dispensing goods and 'transcends itself' in a culture. We are thus taken over at one and the same time by an established agency and by that agency's self-image.

The Logic of Father Christmas

Those who pooh-pooh the ability of advertising and of the mass media in general to condition people have failed to grasp the peculiar logic upon which the media's efficacy reposes. For this is not a logic of propositions and proofs, but a logic of fables and of the willingness to go along with them. We do not believe in such fables, but we cleave to them nevertheless. Basically, the 'demonstration' of a product convinces no one, but it does serve to rationalize its purchase, which in any case either precedes or overwhelms all rational motives. Without 'believing' in the product, therefore, *we believe in the advertising that tries to get us to believe in it.* We are for all the world like children in their attitude towards Father Christmas. Children hardly ever wonder whether Father Christmas exists or not, and they certainly never look upon getting presents as an effect of which that existence is the cause: rather, their belief in Father Christmas is a rationalizing confabulation designed to extend earliest infancy's miraculously gratifying relationship with the parents (and particularly with the mother) into a later stage of childhood. That miraculous relationship, though now in actuality past, is internalized in the form of a belief which is in effect an ideal extension of it. There is nothing artificial about the romance of Father Christmas, however, for it is based upon the shared interest that the two parties involved have in its preservation. Father Christmas himself is unimportant here, and the child only believes in him precisely because of that basic lack of significance. What children are actually consuming through this figure, fiction or cover story (which in a sense they continue to believe in even after they have ceased to do so) is the action of a magical parental solicitude and the care taken by the parents to continue colluding with their children's embrace of the fable. Christmas presents themselves serve merely to underwrite this compromise.[21]

Advertising functions in much the same way. Neither its rhetoric nor even the informational aspect of its discourse has a decisive effect on the buyer. What the individual does respond to, on the other hand, is advertising's underlying leitmotiv of protection and gratification, the intimation that its solicitations and attempts to persuade are the sign, indecipherable at the

---

21. One is reminded of the neutral substances or placebos that doctors sometimes prescribe for psychosomatic patients. Quite often these patients make just as good a recovery after the administration of such inactive elements as they do after taking real medicine. What is it that such patients derive or assimilate from the placebo? The answer is the idea of medicine *plus* the presence of the physician: the mother and the father simultaneously. Here too, then, belief facilitates the retrieval of an infantile situation, the result being the regressive resolution of a psychosomatic conflict.

conscious level, that somewhere there is an agency (a social agency in the event, but one that refers directly to the image of the mother) which has taken it upon itself to inform him of his own desires, and to foresee and rationalize these desires to his own satisfaction. He thus no more 'believes' in advertising than the child believes in Father Christmas, but this in no way impedes his capacity to embrace an internalized infantile situation, and to act accordingly. Herein lies the very real effectiveness of advertising, founded on its obedience to a logic which, though not that of the conditioned reflex, is nonetheless very rigorous: a logic of belief and regression.[22]

Society as Maternal Agency: Airborne's Armchair

Sometimes this mythology is quite explicit in the discourse of advertising.[23] Consider a flyer put out by Airborne, specialists in armchairs, sofas and seating in general. 'True Comfort Cannot Be Improvised', runs the title. We are being warned here against the easy solution: comfort is not passivity, but has to be actively 'created' if passivity is to become possible. The text which follows immediately stresses Airborne's modern and scientific virtues:

> A good seat is a combination of four different factors: aesthetics, comfort, sturdiness and finish. . . . The creation of a master-piece of this kind calls for something beyond the skills of the traditional craftsman. Not that those skills are now dispensable; on the contrary, they still lie at the very heart of the furniture maker's trade. . . .

The past is thus the guarantee of a kind of moral security: tradition is at once preserved and surpassed by the industrial revolution. But

22. Such an approach might well be extended to mass communications in general, though this is not the place to attempt it.
23. This is by no means necessary, however – the advertising image alone can easily convey it.

'in this day and age a good seat has to be manufactured according to the means and methods decreed by the economics of the modern world'. In other words, this armchair cannot be just an armchair. Its purchaser must feel himself at one with a technological society (a society, of course, whose norms are nevertheless kept secret from him). The armchair makes him into a citizen of industrial society.

> This company, now meeting the comfort needs of thousands of French households, has become an entire industry in its own right, complete with its own research departments, engineers and creative artists, not to mention its machines, its stocks of raw materials, its after-sales service agencies, its sales network, etc.

The consumer needs to be fully aware that the industrial revolution took place for his benefit, that today all the structures of society are embodied in the qualities of this armchair, qualities which themselves come together in his own individual personality. In this way a whole universe is constituted which from his point of view is governed by the sole sublime aim of ensuring his satisfaction. This perspective is confirmed as Airborne's advertising copy continues: 'A good armchair is a seat in which every family member feels at ease. There is no need to adjust it to your weight or height, for it is designed to wed the shape of your body.' There is no need to change anything in society or in yourself, because the industrial revolution has occurred, and technological society in its entirety adapts itself to you via this armchair so perfectly matched to your body's contours. There was a time when moral norms demanded that the individual adapt to society at large, but from the standpoint of an age of consumption – or a would-be age of consumption – such requirements belong to the outmoded ideology of the age of production; nowadays it is society as a whole which must adapt to the individual. What is more, society does not merely estimate the individual's needs and adapt to this or that particular need; rather, it is at pains to adapt to the individual himself, personally: 'You can always tell an Airborne seat from the fact that, when you sit in it, it is always YOUR armchair, YOUR chair or YOUR sofa, and you always get that comfortable feeling of being in a seat made exactly to measure for you alone.' To put all this metasociology of compliance in a nutshell: by virtue of this armchair's devotion, submissiveness and secret affinities with you personally, you will come to believe also in the devotion of Airborne's owner, his technical services, and so on and so forth. In this armchair, which is frankly quite pleasant to sit in (it is truly very functional), you are thus expected to apprehend the essence of a society that is definitively civilized, a society irreversibly committed to the idea of happiness – to YOUR happiness – and a society that spontaneously supplies each of its members with the wherewithal to achieve their own self-realization.

This ideological discourse extends even to consideration of materials and forms. Airborne's advertising evokes 'new materials which effectively embody the style of today'. 'After the Stone Age and the Age of Wood, we are now living, as far as furnishing is concerned, in the Steel Age.' 'Steel provides the structure.' And so on. But though steel may be exciting, it is also a rather hard substance, rather too closely associated with effort, with the necessity for the individual to adapt. So, sure enough, it has to be hastily transfigured, rendered pliant – the 'structure' has to be humanized:

> Though solid and unyielding, steel is suppleness itself when it is transformed into a set of springs. Once overlaid with genuine latex foam, it is soft and comfortable. And aesthetic too – because it may be wedded perfectly [again!] with the warmth of today's fabrics.

Structure is always violent, and distressingly so. Even at the level of the object it threatens to compromise the individual's relationship to society. To pacify reality, an appearance of peacefulness must be preserved. In order to please you, the Airborne armchair is thus transmuted by a seemingly natural process from steel to fabric, becoming a mirror of strength and tranquillity. And of course, to complete the picture, 'aesthetics' envelops 'structure', and celebrates the definitive wedding of the object to your 'personality'. Here again a rhetoric of substances is the vehicle of social conditioning. In this structure become form, in this quieted tenacity, in this ubiquitous 'nuptial' synthesis with its interplay between contentment and the memory of a will, in this phallic phantasy of violence (steel) which is, as it were, calmed and lulled by its own image – surely it is impossible not to discern, in all these, a pattern of global collusion with the world, implying a complete resolution of all tensions in a maternal and harmonious society.

It is not, therefore, that advertising 'alienates' or 'mystifies' us with its claims, words or images; rather, we are swayed by the fact that 'they' are sufficiently concerned to want to address us, to show us things, to take an interest in us. Riesman[24] and other critical theorists of American society have clearly shown how products are increasingly judged not by their intrinsic value but instead by the concern for one's existence that they imply on the part of the manufacturer, by the solicitude the advertiser demonstrates for the public.[25] Individuals are gradually conditioned by their ceaseless consumption – at once gratifying and frustrating, glorious and guilt-inducing – of the social body in its totality.

What advertising bestows upon objects, the quality without which 'they would not be what they are', is 'warmth'. Warmth is

24. *The Lonely Crowd* (see above, p. 152, note 17), pp. 210 ff.
25. In the case of radio programmes sponsored by a particular product, for example, the advertising injunction itself may be quite minimal as compared with the emotional collusion involved; indeed, it may amount to no more than a statement of the type 'This programme comes to you courtesy of Brand X'.

a modern property which we have already identified as the basis of 'atmosphere': just as colours are hot or cold (rather than red or green); just as the 'controlling dimension of personality'[26] (in an 'other-directed' society) is the 'warm-cold axis'; so likewise objects are hot or cold, that is to say, indifferent and hostile, or spontaneous, sincere and communicative – in a word, they are 'personalized'. They no longer present themselves as appropriate to some strictly circumscribed task – a crude and outdated practice; instead they submit themselves to us, they seek us out, surround us, and prove their existence to us by virtue of the profusion of ways in which they appear, by virtue of their effusiveness. We are taken as the object's aims, and the object *loves* us. And because we are loved, we feel that we exist: we are 'personalized'. This is the essential thing – the actual purchase of the object is secondary. The abundance of products puts an end to *scarcity*; the abundance of advertising puts an end to *insecurity*. The worst thing possible is to be obliged to invent one's own motives for acting, for preferring, for buying. The individual in such circumstances is inevitably brought face to face with his own misapprehensions, his own lack of existence, his own bad faith and anxiety. Any object which fails to dispel such guilty feelings – which fails, as it were, to know what I want, and what I am – is liable to be dubbed bad.[27] If the object loves me, then shall I be saved. Advertising (and, more broadly, public relations as a whole) relieves psychological insecurity by deploying an enormous solicitude, to which we respond by internalizing the solicitous agency – namely, that whole immense enterprise, producing not just goods but also communicational warmth, which global consumer society actually is.

26. Riesman, *The Lonely Crowd*, p. 167.
27. Thus Riesman tells us of a Chicago suburb whose residents protest, not against any objective short-comings of the municipal services, but rather against the deficiencies of the psychological support offered, complaining that they have been 'so manipulated as to make them "not like it"' (ibid., p. 213).

We should remember, too, that in a society where everything is strictly subject to the laws of selling and profit, advertising is the most democratic of products, the only one that is 'free' – and 'free' to all. Objects are always sold; only advertising is offered gratis.[28] The mechanism of advertising thus subtly renews links with archaic rituals of giving, of offering presents, as well as with the infantile situation of a passive gratification vouchsafed by the parents. Both choice and advertising serve to transform a purely commercial relationship into a personal one.[29]

The Festival of Buying Power

This gratificatory, infantilizing function of advertising, which is the basis of our belief in it and hence of our collusion with the social entity, is equally well illustrated by its playful aspect. We are certainly susceptible to the reassurance advertising offers by supplying an image that is never negative, but we are equally affected by advertising as a fantastic manifestation of a society capable of swamping the mere necessity of products in superfluous images: advertising as a show (again, the most democratic of all), a game, a *mise en scène*. Advertising serves as a permanent display of the buying power, be it real or virtual, of society overall. Whether we partake of it personally or not, we all live and breathe this buying power. By virtue of advertising, too, the product exposes itself to our view and invites us to handle it; it is, in fact, eroticized

28. The same goes for *choice* (see 'Models and Series' above): the object *per se* is sold to us, but the 'range' of objects on offer is 'free'.
29. That choice and advertising should be offered to us 'free' in this way results from a greater expenditure on the 'personalization' of models and on the dissemination of advertising than on basic technical research. What is given to us 'free' at the psychological level takes away from the technical qualities of what is being sold to us. The significance of this tendency can hardly be understated, and in 'developed' societies it has assumed truly vast proportions. At the same time, who is to say whether advertising, by relieving insecurity and satisfying the imagination, does not fulfil an *objective* function every bit as fundamental as a technical progress responding to material needs?

– not just because of the explicitly sexual themes evoked[30] but also because the purchase itself, simple appropriation, is transformed into a manoeuvre, a scenario, a complicated dance which endows a purely practical transaction with all the traits of amorous dalliance: advances, rivalry, obscenity, flirtation, prostitution – even irony. The mechanics of buying (which is already libidinally charged) gives way to a complete eroticization of choosing and spending.[31] Our modern environment assails us relentlessly, especially in the cities, with its lights and its images, its incessant inducements to status-consciousness and narcissism, emotional involvement and obligatory relationships. We live in a cold-blooded carnival atmosphere, a formal yet electrifying ambience of empty sensual gratification wherein the actual process of buying and consuming is demonstrated, illuminated, mimicked – even frustrated – much as the sexual act is anticipated by dance. By means of advertising, as once upon a time by means of feasts, society puts itself on display and consumes its own image.

An essential regulatory function is evident here. Like the dream, advertising defines and redirects an imaginary potentiality. Like the dream's, its practical character is strictly subjective and individual.[32] And, like the dream, advertising is devoid of all negativity and relativity: with never a sign too many nor a sign too few, it is essentially superlative and totally immanent in nature.[33] Our night-time dreams are uncaptioned, whereas the one that we

30. Some common leitmotivs (breasts, lips) should perhaps be deemed less erotic than 'nurturing' in character.
31. The literal meaning of the German word for advertising, '*die Werbung*', is erotic exploration. '*Der unworbene Mensch*', the person won over by advertising, can also mean a person who is sexually solicited.
32. Advertising campaigns designed to alter group behaviour or modify social structures (for example, those against alcohol abuse, dangerous driving, etc.) are notoriously ineffective. Advertising resists the (collective) reality principle. The only imperative that may be effective in this context is 'Give!' – for it is part of the reversible system of gratification.
33. Negative or ironic advertisements are mere antiphrasis – a well-known device, too, of the dream.

live in our waking hours via the city's hoardings, in our newspapers and on our screens, is covered with captions, with multiple subtitling. Both, however, weave the most colourful of narratives from the most impoverished of raw materials, and just as the function of nocturnal dreams is to protect sleep, so likewise the prestige of advertising and consumption serves to ensure the spontaneous absorption of ambient social values and the regression of the individual into social consensus.

Festival, immanence, positivity – to use such terms amounts to saying that *in the first instance advertising is itself less a determinant of consumption than an object of consumption.* What would an object be today if it were not put on offer both in the mode of discourse and image (advertising) and in the mode of a range of models (choice)? It would be psychologically nonexistent. And what would modern citizens be if objects and products were not proposed to them in the twin dimensions of advertising and choice? They would not be *free.* We can understand the reactions of the two thousand West Germans polled by the Allenbach Demoscopic Institute: 60 per cent expressed the view that there was too much advertising, yet when they were asked, 'Would you rather have too much advertising (Western style) or minimal – and only socially useful – advertising (as in the East)?', a majority favoured the first of these options, taking an excess of advertising as indicative not only of affluence but also of freedom – and hence of a basic value.[34] Such is the measure of the emotional and ideological collusion that advertising's spectacular mediation creates between the individual and society (whatever the structures of the latter may be). If all advertising were abolished, individuals would feel frustrated by the empty hoardings. Frustrated not merely by the lack of opportunity (even in an ironic way) for play, for dreaming, but also, more profoundly, by the feeling that

34. Naturally the existing political situation of the two Germanies must be taken into account, but there can be little doubt that the absence of advertising in the Western sense is a real contributing factor to West German prejudice against the East.

they were no longer somehow 'being taken care of'. They would miss an environment thanks to which, in the absence of active social participation, they can at least partake of a travesty of the social entity and enjoy a warmer, more maternal and more vivid atmosphere. One of the first demands of man in his progression towards well-being is that his desires be attended to, that they be formulated and expressed in the form of images for his own contemplation (something which is a problem, or becomes a problem, in socialist countries). Advertising fills this function, which is futile, regressive and inessential – yet for that very reason even more profoundly necessary.

Gratification/Repression: A Two-Sided Agency

We need to discern the true imperative of advertising behind the gentle litany of the object: 'Look how the whole of society simply adapts itself to you and your desires. It is therefore only reasonable that you should become integrated into that society.' Persuasion is hidden, as Vance Packard says, but its aim is less the 'compulsion' to buy, or conditioning by means of objects, than the subscription to social consensus that this discourse urges: the object is a service, a personal relationship between society and you. Whether advertising is organized around the image of the mother or around the need to play, it always aims to foster *the same tendency to regress to a point anterior to real social processes*, such as work, production, the market, or value, which might disturb this magical integration: the object has not been bought by you, you have voiced a desire for it and all the engineers, technicians, and so on, have worked to gratify your desire. With the advent of industrial society the division of labour severs labour from its product. Advertising adds the finishing touch to this development by creating a radical split, at the moment of purchase, between *products* and consumer *goods*; by interpolating a vast maternal image between labour and the product of labour, it causes that *product* no longer to be viewed as such (complete with its history, and so on), but purely and simply as a good, as an *object*. And even as it separates the producer and the consumer within the one individual, thanks to the material abstraction of a highly differentiated system of objects, advertising strives inversely to re-create the infantile confusion of the object with the desire for the object, to return the consumer to the stage at which the infant makes no distinction between its mother and what its mother gives it.

In reality advertising's careful omission of objective processes and the social history of objects is simply a way of making it easier, by means of the imagination as a social agency, to impose the *real* order of production and exploitation. This is where, behind the psychogogy of advertising, it behoves us to recognize the demagogy of a *political* discourse whose own tactics are founded on a splitting into two – on the splitting of social reality into a real agency and an image, with the first disappearing behind the second, becoming indecipherable and giving way to nothing more than a pattern of absorption into a maternal world. When advertising tells you, in effect, that 'society adapts itself totally to you, so integrate yourself totally into society', the reciprocity thus invoked is obviously fake: what adapts to you is an imaginary agency, whereas you are asked in exchange to adapt to an agency that is distinctly real. Via the armchair that 'weds the shape of your body', it is the entire technical and political order of society that weds *you* and takes you in hand. Society assumes a maternal role the better to preserve the rule of *constraint*.[35] The immense political role played by the diffusion of products and advertising techniques is here clearly evident: these mechanisms effectively replace earlier moral or political ideologies. Indeed, they go farther, for moral and political forms of integration were never unproblematical and always had to be buttressed by overt repression,

35. What is more, behind this system of gratification we may discern the reinforcement of all the structures of authority (planning, centralization, bureaucracy). Parties, States, power structures – all are able to strengthen their hegemony under cover of this immense mother-image which renders any real challenge to them less and less possible.

whereas the new techniques manage to do without any such assistance: the consumer internalizes the agency of social control and its norms in the very process of consuming.

This effectiveness is reinforced by the status accorded the signs advertising manipulates and the process whereby these are 'read'.

Signs in advertising speak to us of objects, but they never (or scarcely ever) explain those objects from the standpoint of a *praxis*: they refer to objects as to a world that is absent. These signs are literally no more than a 'legend': they are there primarily for the purpose of being read. But while they do not refer to the real world, neither do they exactly replace that world: their function is to impose a specific activity, a specific kind of reading. If they did carry information, then a *full* reading, and a transition to the practical realm, would occur. But their role is a different one: to draw attention to the absence of what they designate. To this extent the reading of such signs is intransitive – organized in terms of a specific system of *satisfaction* which is, however, perpetually determined by the absence of reality, that is to say, by *frustration*.

The image creates a void, indicates an absence, and it is in this respect that it is 'evocative'. It is deceptive, however. It provokes a cathexis which it then immediately short-circuits at the level of reading. It focuses free-floating wishes upon an object which it masks as much as reveals. The image disappoints: *its function is at once to display and simultaneously to disabuse*. Looking is based on a presumption of contact; the image and its reading are based on a presumption of possession. Thus advertising offers neither a hallucinated satisfaction nor a practical mediation with the world. Rather, what it produces is dashed hopes: unfinished actions, continual initiatives followed by continual abandonments thereof, false dawnings of objects, false dawnings of desires. A whole psychodrama is quickly enacted when an image is read. In principle, this enables the reader to assume his passive role and be transformed into a consumer. In actuality, the sheer profusion of images works at the same time to counter any shift in the direction of reality, subtly to fuel feelings of guilt by means of continual frustration, and to arrest consciousness at the level of a phantasy of satisfaction. In the end the image and the reading of the image are by no means the shortest way to the object, merely the shortest way to another image. The signs of advertising thus follow upon one another like the transient images of hypnagogic states.

We must not forget that the image serves in this way to avoid reality and create frustration, for only thus can we grasp how it is that *the reality principle omitted from the image nevertheless effectively re-emerges therein as the continual repression of desire* (as the spectacularization, blocking and dashing of that desire and, ultimately, its regressive and visible transference onto an object). This is where the profound collusion between the advertising sign and the overall order of society becomes most evident: it is not in any mechanical sense that advertising conveys the values of society; rather, more subtly, it is in its ambiguous *presumptive* function – somewhere between possession and dispossession, at once a designation and an indication of absence – that the advertising sign 'inserts' the social order into its system of simultaneous determination by gratification on the one hand and repression on the other.[36]

Gratification, frustration – two indivisible aspects of social integration. Every advertising image is a key, a *legend*, and as such reduces the anxiety-provoking polysemy of the world. But in the name of intelligibility the image becomes impoverished, cursory; inasmuch as it is still susceptible of too many interpretations, its meaning is further narrowed by the addition of

36. This account may also be applied to the system of objects. Because the object too is ambiguous, because it is never *merely* an object but always at the same time *an indication of the absence of a human relationship* (just as the sign in advertising is an indication of the absence of a real object) – for these reasons, the object may like-wise play a powerful integrative role. It is true, however, that the object's practical specificity means that the indication of the absence of the real is less marked in the case of the object than in that of the advertising sign.

discourse – of a subtitle, as it were, which constitutes a second legend. And, by virtue of the way it is read, the image always refers only to other images. In the end advertising soothes people's consciousness by means of a controlled social semantics – controlled, ultimately, to the point of focusing on a single referent, namely the whole society itself. Society thus monopolizes all the roles. It conjures up a host of images whose meanings it immediately strives to limit. It generates an anxiety that it then seeks to calm. It fulfils and disappoints, mobilizes and demobilizes. Under the banner of advertising it institutes the reign of a freedom of desire, but desire is never truly liberated thereby (which would in fact entail the end of the social order): desire is liberated by the image only to the point where its emergence triggers the associated reflexes of anxiety and guilt. Primed by the image only to be defused by it, and made to feel guilty to boot, the nascent desire is co-opted by the agency of control. There is a profusion of freedom, but this freedom is imaginary; a continual mental orgy, but one which is stage-managed, a controlled regression in which all perversity is resolved in favour of order. If gratification is massive in consumer society, repression is equally massive – and both reach us together via the images and discourse of advertising, which activate the repressive reality principle at the very heart of the pleasure principle.

The Presumption of Collectivity

Pax Washing Powder

It is not only the objective processes of production and of the market that are passed over in silence by advertising, but also real society and its contradictions. Advertising plays on the presence/absence of an overall social body – on a *presumption of collectivity*. The collective realm is imaginary in advertising, but its virtual consumption suffices to ensure serial conditioning. Take, for instance, a poster for Pax Washing Powder. We are shown an immense faceless crowd waving immaculate white flags (Pax whiteness) and gazing towards an idol in their midst consisting of a gigantic carton of Pax, reproduced with photographic accuracy, whose size relative to the crowd is approximately that of the United Nations building in New York. Of course a whole ideology of honesty and peace underpins this image, but for our present purposes the most interesting thing here is the way it makes use of a hypostasized collectivity. The individual consumer will be successfully persuaded that he personally desires Pax to the extent that his own image is reflected back to him in advance as part of a synthesis. The crowd in the advertisement is him, and his desire is evoked by the image's presumption of a collective desire. Advertising is very canny here, for every desire, no matter how intimate, still aspires to universality. Subtending a man's desire for a woman is the assumption that all men are capable of desiring her. No desire, even a sexual one, can endure without the mediation of an imagined collective realm. Perhaps, indeed, no desire can ever take form without this imaginary dimension: is it conceivable that a man could love a woman if he were certain that no other man in the world could possibly desire her? Conversely, one can easily love a woman one does not even know if she is adored by masses of people. This is the ever-present (but for the most part hidden) underpinning of advertising. It is normal that our desires as we experience them should embody a reference to the collectivity, but what advertising strives to do is to make this the inaugural dimension of desire. Far from relying on the spontaneity of individual needs, advertising prefers to control these needs by mobilizing the collective reference and having consciousness crystallize entirely upon the collective idea. There is a kind of totalitarian social dynamics here, jubilantly celebrating its finest victory – the successful prosecution of a strategy of solicitation founded on the presumption of collectivity. This promotion of desire on the sole basis of the group responds to a fundamental need, that of communication, but it does so as a way of reinforcing not genuine collectivity but merely a phantom thereof. The Pax advertisement is perfectly clear: advertising affects to unify individuals on the basis of a product whose purchase and use actually banish each individual to his own private sphere. Paradoxically we are induced, in the name of everyone and out of a reflex of solidarity, to buy an object that we immediately use to differentiate ourselves from other people. Thus *nostalgia for collectivity fuels competition between individuals.* In point of fact this competition is itself illusory, in that in the end each individual who first reads the poster and then buys the product is *personally* buying *the same object* as everyone else. The upshot of the transaction, its 'benefit' (to the social order), remains a regressive identification with a vague collective totality, and hence an internalization of the sanction of the social group. As always, complicity and guilt are closely associated here: what advertising *also* underpins, therefore, is (virtual) guilt towards the group. But it no longer does so according to the traditional pattern of moral censure, the difference being that anxiety and guilt are now aroused in advance, ready for use as required; and in fact they will be used, with the emergence of a controlled desire, to effect submission to group norms. It may be easy enough to resist the explicit imperative of the Pax poster – to declare that it cannot make you buy Pax rather than Omo or Sunil or, for that matter, any of them; it is much harder to reject the poster's second referent, namely the vibrant and enthusiastic crowd (buttressed by the ideology of 'peace'). And the reason why we have difficulty resisting this pattern of complicity is that here *resistance is not even the issue*: it is true that in this particular advertisement the connotation is still easy to interpret, but group sanction need not be indicated by a crowd: any representation whatsoever will do. An erotic one, for instance. True, we do not buy potato crisps *just because* they are connoted by a woman with blonde hair and a sexy bottom. What is certain, though, is that the brief moment when the libido is thus mobilized by an image offers a sufficient opportunity for society as an agency of control to invade us in its entirety, complete with its customary armamentarium, namely the mechanisms of repression, sublimation and transference.

Promotional Contests

Every year certain newspapers feature long-running competitions that conclude with the following decisive question: 'How many correct solutions will we receive in this contest?' The function of this simple question is to reintroduce pure chance, to whose elimination the contestants have by now been applying their minds for several weeks. Any real competition is thus immediately reduced to the kind of magical choosing that characterizes lotteries. What is interesting, however, is that the chance involved here is of no ordinary kind. It is neither the God nor the fate of earlier times, but a nonce-collectivity, a contingent and arbitrary group (the sum total of people liable to enter or win the contest) which becomes the agency of adjudication, and it is the divining of this agency, the successful identification of an individual with this collective chance, that becomes the mark of the winner. All of which explains why the earlier questions in such competitions are generally so simple: the greatest possible number of entrants have to participate in the essential moment, in the magical intuiting of the Great Collectivity (pure chance serves, in addition, to restore the myth of absolute democracy). In short, the ultimate referent of these competitions turns out to be a sort of phantom collectivity, purely conjectural in nature, non-structural, devoid of any image of itself (it is 'embodied' solely in the most abstract way, and simultaneously with its self-dissolution, in the number of correct entries received), and bound up exclusively with the gratification of the single person or very few people who have happed upon it in its very abstractness.

Garap

We consume the product through the product itself, but we consume its meaning through advertising. Picture for a moment our modern cities stripped of all signs, their walls blank as an empty consciousness. And imagine that all of a sudden the single word GARAP appears everywhere, written on every wall. A pure signifier, having no referent, signifying only itself, it is read, discussed, interpreted in a vacuum, signified despite itself – in short, consumed *qua* sign. What indeed can it signify except for the society itself that is capable of generating such a sign? By virtue of its very lack of signification it mobilizes an entire imaginary collectivity. It comes to stand for a whole society. In a way people end up 'believing' in GARAP. They consider it the mark of advertising's omnipotence, and judge that if only GARAP would assume the specificity of a product, then that product would meet with an immediate and sweeping success. Nothing, however, could be less certain, and the cunning of the advertisers lies precisely in the fact that they never reveal this. Were a specific referent to be made explicit, individual resistance would certainly come back into play. But consent (even ironic consent) thus founded on faith in a pure sign is self-creating. Advertising's true referent is here apparent in its purest form: like GARAP, advertising is mass society itself, using systematic, arbitrary signs to arouse emotions and mobilize consciousness, and reconstituting its collective nature in this very process.[37]

Advertising is a plebiscite whereby mass consumer society wages a perpetual campaign of self-endorsement.[38]

37. Every single advertising sign bears independent witness to this tautological system of recognition, because all such signs, whatever they signify, also refer to themselves *as advertising*.
38. Is this not somewhat reminiscent of Claude Lévi-Strauss's account of the totemic system, according to which arbitrary totemic signs are the conduit by whose means a social order makes itself apparent in its durable immanence? Viewed in this light, advertising would appear to be the end-product of a cultural system which has reverted (with its repertoire of 'brands') to the poverty of the sign codes of archaic systems.

A New Humanism?

Serial Conditioning

It should now be easier to grasp the nature of the system of conditioning that is at work behind the themes of competition and 'personalization'. That same ideology of competition which formerly, under the banner of 'freedom', constituted the golden rule of production has now been transposed without restrictions into the realm of consumption. Thanks to thousands of marginal distinctions and the often purely formal diffraction of a single product by means of conditioning, competition has become more aggravated on every plane, opening up the immense range of possibilities of a precarious freedom – indeed, of the ultimate freedom, namely the freedom to choose the objects which will distinguish one from other people.[39] In fact the ideology of competition is arguably bound to fall here into the toils of the same process, and hence to meet the same fate, as it did in the realm of production: although consumption may still take itself for a sort of liberal progression in which personal expression has a part to play, whereas production is inescapably governed by planning, this is merely because the techniques of psychological conditioning are far less advanced than those of economic planning.

We in Europe still want what others do not have: in the West, at any rate (the question having been deferred in the Eastern bloc), we are still at the competitive, the heroic stage in the choice and use of objects. The regular replacement and cyclical synchronization of models have not yet established themselves here as they have in the

39. The French word '*concurrence*' [here rendered as 'competition' – *Trans.*] is ambiguous in that it means both rivalry and convergence. It is true that furious competition is a sure way to produce convergence at a single point. There is a threshold of technical progress (reached notably in the United States) beyond which all objects of a given type become interchangeable, and the differentiation requirement can then be fulfilled only to the extent that all are modified in unison, say once a year, and this in accordance with the same criteria. The extreme form of free choice similarly subjects everyone to the ritual obligation to possess the same things.

United States.[40] Should we attribute this to psychological resistance, or perhaps to the strength of tradition? Probably the cause is a simpler one: the majority of Western Europe's population is still a long way from achieving the sort of economic status that makes it fundamentally possible, with all objects of consumption aligned on the same maximal standard, for a single repertoire of models to hold sway, for diversity to become in effect less important than owning the 'latest' model, which is the essential stamp of social worth. In the United States 90 per cent of the population aspire solely to the possession of what others possess, and from one year to the next they massively choose the latest model, which is in every single respect the best. A solid class of 'normal' consumers has thus been constituted which, for all practical purposes, coincides with the entire population. Although we have not yet reached that stage in Europe, we are already very well able, on account of the irreversible pressure exerted by the American model, to perceive the ambiguity of advertising: it *provokes us into competing*, but at the same time the imaginary competition thus set in motion *already bespeaks a profound monotony*, a demand for uniformity, the sinking of the consuming masses into a regressive contentment. It tells us to 'Buy this, because it is like nothing else' ('the meat of the elite', 'the cigarette of the happy few', etc.) – but it also tells us to 'Buy this because everyone else uses it!'[41] Nor is there any real contradiction here. It is quite possible for each

40. In the United States, essential objects such as cars and refrigerators tend to have a predictable and obligatory life-span of one year (three years in the case of television sets, somewhat longer for a flat). Norms of social status end up imposing a kind of metabolism of the object, an ever-accelerating cycle. Very far removed from the cycles of nature, yet often oddly congruent with the old round of the seasons, this new kind of cycle and the necessity of complying with it are now the true basis of the American citizen's ethos.
41. This ambiguity is perfectly epitomized by advertising's use of 'you' – as in 'Guinness is Good for You'. Is this a polite (and hence personalizing) way of addressing the individual, or is the message directed at the social group as a whole? Is this 'you' (or the French *vous* in similar contexts) singular or plural? The answer is both: the pronoun addresses each individual inasmuch as he resembles all others. Fundamentally this is the impersonal or gnomic 'you' (cf. Leo Spitzer in *Sprache im technischen Zeitalter*, December 1964, p. 961).

person to feel unique even though everyone is alike: all that is needed is a pattern of collective and mythological projection – in other words, a model.[42]

We may well conclude that the destiny of consumer society (thanks not to Machiavellian technocrats but, rather, to the simple structural play of competition) is the functionalization of the consumer himself, the psychological monopolization of all needs – a unanimity in consumption which will at last harmonize with the concentration and unbridled interventionism that govern production.

Freedom by Default

Moreover, the ideology of competition is now giving way everywhere to a 'philosophy' of personal accomplishment. Society is better integrated, so instead of vying for possession of things, individuals seek self-fulfilment, independently of one another, through what they consume. The leitmotiv of discriminative competition has been replaced by that of personalization for all. Meanwhile, advertising has transformed itself from a commercial practice into a theory of the *praxis* of consumption, a theory which now crowns the whole social edifice. Expositions of this theory are to be found in the works of American advertising men (Ernest Dichter, Pierre Martineau, *et alii*). The thesis is simple: (1) the consumer society (objects, products, advertising) offers the individual the possibility, for the first time in history, of total liberation and self-realization; (2) transcending consumption pure and simple in the direction of individual and collective self-expression, the system of consumption constitutes a true language,

42. When Brigitte Bardot hairdos were all the rage, every girl who followed the fashion remained unique in her own eyes, because her point of reference was never the thousands of others who looked exactly like her but, rather, Bardot herself, sublime archetype and fountainhead of uniqueness. Among the mad – to carry this logic to its extreme – there is nothing especially bothersome about being one of four or five people in the asylum all of whom take themselves for Napoleon. Consciousness here is shaped not by a real relationship but by an imaginary one.

a new culture. The 'nihilism' of consumption is thus effectively countered by a 'new humanism' of consumption.

As to the first point, the question of personal fulfilment, Ernest Dichter, director of the Institute for Motivational Research, does not hesitate to define the problematics of the 'new man' as follows:

> The problem confronting us now is how to allow the average American to feel moral even when he is flirting, even when he is spending money, even when he is buying a second or third car. One of the most difficult tasks created by our current affluence is sanctioning and justifying people's enjoyment of it, convincing them that to take pleasure in their lives is moral and not immoral. Permission given the consumer freely to enjoy life, and proof that he has the right to surround himself with products that enrich his existence and give him pleasure – these should be the cardinal themes of all advertising and of all attempts to promote sales.[43]

The manipulating of motivation thus apparently ushers in an era in which advertising will assume moral responsibility for society as a body, replacing puritanical morality with a hedonism founded purely on satisfaction and introducing a new state of nature, so to speak, into the bosom of hypercivilization. There is an ambivalence in Dichter's last sentence, however: is the goal of advertising to free man from his resistance to happiness, or is it to promote sales? Is society to be reorganized for the sake of satisfaction or for the sake of profits? In his preface to the French edition of Vance Packard's *The Hidden Persuaders*, Marcel Bleustein-Blanchet maintains that 'motivational research is no threat to individual freedom and in no way prejudices the individual's right to be rational or irrational'. But this claim is simple-minded, if not

43. [*Translator's note*: The author gives *The Strategy of Desire* as the source of this passage, but I have been unable to trace it in the original edition (Garden City, NY: Doubleday, 1960), so I have retranslated from the French. But see the identical arguments set forth in Dichter's book, pp. 253 ff.]

disingenuous. Dichter is more frank, and makes it clear that the freedom in question is *conceded*. He talks of 'giving consumers permission' – in other words, people must be allowed to be children without being ashamed of it. 'Free to be oneself' really means free to project one's desires onto commodities. And Dichter's 'free to enjoy life' means free to be irrational and regressive – and hence adapted to a specific social organization of production.[44] The 'philosophy' of selling has little use for such paradoxes, and it appeals to rational goals (enlightening people as to what they want) and to scientific methods as justifications for its attempt to provoke irrational behaviour (i.e. accepting the role of being nothing but a bundle of unmediated drives and being satisfied so long as those drives are satisfied). Even drives can be dangerous, however, and the neo-sorcerers of consumption are very careful indeed not to liberate anybody with a rousing call to happiness. Rather, they offer merely to resolve tensions – that is to say, they offer a freedom merely *by default*:

> . . . whenever a person in one socioeconomic category aspires
> to a different category, a 'tension differential' is developed
> within him and this leads to frustration and action. Where a
> product promises to help a group overcome this tension,
> achieve its level of aspiration in whatever area it may fall, that
> product has a chance of success.[45]

The aim is to allow drives hitherto inhibited by psychic agencies (taboos, superego, guilt) to crystallize upon objects, which themselves thus become capable of negating the explosive force of desire and materializing the ritual repressive function of the social order. What is dangerous is freedom of being, for it pits the individual against society. Freedom of ownership, however, is harmless, for it

44. Adapting a Marxian formulation from 'On the Jewish Question', we might say that the individual in consumer society is free as a consumer, but only as a consumer. The emancipation involved is a purely formal one.
45. *The Strategy of Desire*, p. 84.

unknowingly serves society's purposes. Such freedom is highly moral, as Dichter points out; indeed, it is the very acme of morality, because it reconciles the consumer with himself and with the group at one and the same time. It is the perfect form of social being. Traditional morality required merely that the individual conform to the group, whereas the philosophy of advertising requires that he conform to himself, that all his personal conflicts be resolved. This is a morality that invades the individual as never before. Taboos, anxieties and neuroses, which tend to make individuals into outsiders and outlaws, are thus supposed to be removed in favour of a reassuring regression into objects calculated to buttress the images of the Father and the Mother in every possible way. The increasingly 'free' irrationality of drives in the depths is to be accompanied by an increasingly strict control as they emerge into the light.

A New Language?

Let us now consider the second claim mentioned above: does the system of objects-cum-advertising really constitute a language? The whole philosophy of idealized consumption is based on the replacement of live, conflictual human relationships by a 'personalized' relationship to objects. 'Any buying process', Pierre Martineau tells us, 'is an interaction between the personality of the individual and the so-called "personality" of the product itself.'[46] The pretence is that products are now so differentiated and so numerous that they have been transformed into *complex* beings, and that consequently the relationship involved in buying and consuming is equivalent to any *human* relationship.[47] But this

46. *Motivation in Advertising: Motives That Make People Buy* (New York: McGraw-Hill, 1957), p. 73.
47. There are other, archaic, ways of personalizing buying: barter, the second-hand trade (which involves chance), shopping expeditions (which involve patience and an element of play), and so on. The reason I call these forms archaic is that they all assume a passive product and an active buyer. Today all the responsibility for personalization has devolved onto advertising.

is the whole point: is there a living syntax here? Do objects inform needs and structure them in a new way? And, reciprocally, do needs inform new social structures through the mediation of objects and their production? If so, then we may speak of language in this connection; if not, then all this is nothing but the self-serving idealizations of managers.

Structure and Demarcation: Brands

Buying today bears no resemblance to a free or living form of exchange. It is a predetermined operation in which two strictly incompatible systems confront one another, one being the mobile, inconsistent individual, with his needs, his conflicts and his negativity; the other being the codified, classified, discontinuous and relatively consistent system of products in all their positivity. There is no interaction between the two, but there is certainly a forced integration of the system of needs into the system of products. Of course, the net result does constitute a system that signifies as well as a system for procuring satisfaction. But for there to be 'language' there has to be syntax, and in the case of objects of mass consumption all we have is an inventory.

Let me try to explain in more detail. At the stage of craft production, objects reflected the contingency, the uniqueness, of needs. The two systems were adapted to one another, yet their combination lacked coherence – indeed, the only coherence was the relative one of needs, which were mobile and contingent: objective technological progress did not exist. With the advent of the industrial era, manufactured products acquired a new coherence, one bestowed on them by the organization of technology and economic structures, while the system of needs now became less consistent than the system of objects. The latter, by imposing this new coherence, was able to mould a civilization.[48]

48. See Gilbert Simondon, *Du mode d'existence des objets techniques* (Paris: Aubier, 1958), p. 24.

At the same time, as Lewis Mumford notes, 'the machine has replaced an unlimited series of variables' – i.e. objects 'made to measure', adapted to specific needs – 'with a limited number of constraints'.[49] This development does undoubtedly lay the foundations for a new language: internal structuring, simplification, transitions to the bounded and the discontinuous, the constitution of technemes and their growing convergence. And if craft objects may be said to be on a par with words or speech [*parole*], it must be acknowledged that industrial technology institutes a linguistic system [*langue*]. But a linguistic system is not language in the full sense [*langage*]:[50] it is not the material structure of the motorcar that gives that car its voice, but the form, colour, contours, accessories or 'social standing' of the car as an object. And what we have here is a Tower of Babel, for each speaks in its own idiom. Even so, serial production contrives, by means of its calibrated differences and combinatorial variations, to carve out meanings, to generate a repertoire or lexicon of forms and colours via which recurrent modalities of 'speech' can be expressed. But does this amount to a language? No, because this vast paradigm lacks any true syntax. It lacks the rigorous syntax of technology and it lacks the loose syntax of needs, and it wafts back and forth between the two, a sort of two-dimensional repertoire which tends to exhaust its possibilities on the day-to-day level in an immense combinatorial grid of types and models where needs, in their incoherence, are effectively assigned places, but no reciprocal structuring occurs as a result; inasmuch as products are better integrated, it is needs that flow towards them and manage – by cutting themselves into pieces, by becoming discontinuous – to insert themselves, with

49. *Technics and Civilization* (see above, p. 57, note 37), pp. 277–8.
50. [*Translator's note*: No convention having been established on the English rendering of the terms *parole, langue* and *langage*, they are given here in square brackets in the hope that this may assist readers interested in the way the author uses these notoriously slippery Saussurean concepts. See also above, p. 11, note 7.]

difficulty and in arbitrary fashion, into the grid of objects. The fact is that the system of individual needs swamps the world of objects with its utter contingency, yet this contingency is somehow inventoried, classified and demarcated by objects: it thus becomes possible to *control* it – and this, from the socio-economic point of view, is the system's real goal.

If the industrial organization of technology acquires the power to mould our civilization, it does so, then, in a dual and contradictory way: by virtue of its coherence but also by virtue of its incoherence. By virtue, at a 'high level', of its structural (technological) coherence, but also, 'at the base', by virtue of the astructural (but controlled) incoherence of the mechanics of the commercialization of products and the satisfaction of needs. It is clear, therefore, that whereas language, because it is neither consumed nor owned in any true sense by those who speak it, always retains the possibility of access to the 'essential', to a syntax of exchange (structured communication), the system of objects-cum-advertising, for its part, overwhelmed by the inessential, by a destructured universe of needs, can satisfy such needs only in piecemeal fashion and can never found new structures of social exchange.

Here, once again, is Pierre Martineau:

> There is no simple relationship between kinds of buyers and kinds of cars, however. Any human is a complex of many motives . . . [whose] meanings may vary in countless combinations. Nevertheless the different makes and models are seen as helping people give expression to their own personality dimensions.

And Martineau offers several examples of such 'personalization':

> The conservative in car choice and behavior wishes to convey such ideas as dignity, reserve, maturity, seriousness. . . . Another definite series of car personalities is selected by the people

> wanting to make known their middle-of-the-road moderation,
> their being fashionable. . . . Further along the range of per-
> sonalities are the innovators and ultramoderns. . . .[51]

No doubt Martineau is right: this is indeed how people define
themselves by means of their objects. What is also clear, though, is
that those objects do not constitute a real language, but merely a
range of distinguishing marks more or less arbitrarily keyed to a
range of stereotyped personalities. Everything suggests that the
differentiating system of consumption is a powerful tool for
demarcating (1) categories of needs within the consumer himself
which now have but the remotest of relationships with the person
as a living whole; and (2) categories – or 'status groups' – within
society overall which can be identified by means of some particular
set of objects. Hierarchies of products and objects thus come to
play precisely the same role as that formerly played by a range of
distinct values: they become the basis, in short, of the group's
ethos.

Both the aforementioned functions entail the solicitation,
impressment and classification of the personal and social world
– a compulsion, exerted through objects, towards integration
into a hierarchical repertoire with no syntax, that is to say, into
a system of categories that is distinctly not a language. It is as
though there were, not a social dialectic, but a social process of
demarcation by whose means an order is imposed, an order
which in turn dictates a sort of objective fate (materialized in
objects) for each subgroup: in short, a set of pigeonholes
within which relationships can only become more impoverished. Our enthusiastic and devious philosophers of 'motivation' would love to convince themselves, as well as everyone
else, that the reign of objects is still the shortest road to
freedom. As evidence of this they need this spectacular muddle
of needs and satisfactions, this profusion of choices – this

51. *Motivation in Advertising*, p. 75.

whole carnival of supply and demand – whose sheer effervescence creates the illusion of a culture. But let there be no mistake: objects work as *categories of objects* which, in the most tyrannical fashion, define *categories of people* – they police social meaning, and the significations they engender are rigidly controlled. In their proliferation, at once arbitrary and coherent, objects are the best possible vector of a social order that is equally arbitrary and equally coherent, and, under the banner of affluence, they indeed become a most effective material expression of that order.

The concept of 'brand', which is advertising's prime concept, sums up the prospects for a 'language' of consumption rather well. All products (with the exception of perishable foodstuffs) are now offered under brand names. Every product 'worthy of the name' has a brand which may sometimes even become a generic term (e.g. 'frigidaire'). The brand's primary function is to designate a product; its secondary function is to mobilize emotional connotations:

> Actually, in our highly competitive system, few products are able to maintain any technical superiority for long. They must be invested with overtones to individualize them; they must be endowed with richness of associations and imagery; they must have many levels of meaning, if we expect them to be top sellers, if we hope that they will achieve the emotional attachment which shows up as brand loyalty.[52]

The psychological restructuring of the consumer may thus turn on a single word – PHILIPS, OLIDA or GENERAL MOTORS – capable of connoting at once a diversity of objects and a mass of diffuse meanings: a synthetic word covering a synthesis of emotions. Such is the miracle of Martineau's 'psychological label'. And this

52. Ibid., p. 50.

is the only language, ultimately, in which the object speaks to us – the only language that it has invented. Yet the basic lexicon that covers our walls and haunts our consciousness remains strictly asyntactic: different brands succeed one another, are juxtaposed, or replace one another, without articulation or transition; this is an erratic lexical system in which brands devour one another and the lifeblood of each brand is interminable repetition. There can be no more impoverished language than this one, laden with referents yet empty of meaning as it is. It is a language of mere *signals*, and 'brand loyalty' can never, therefore, be more than a conditioned reflex of manipulated emotions.

The philosophers of advertising will doubtless object that the satisfaction of 'deep motives' can only be a good thing (even if these motives are then integrated into an impoverished system of labels). 'Free yourselves from your inner censor!', they are liable to cry. 'Outsmart your superego!' 'Have the courage of your desires!' But the question is: are these deep motives really being called up so that they may be articulated as a language? Can a system of reference such as this really invest hitherto hidden areas of the personality with meaning – and, if so, with what meaning? To quote Martineau one last time:

> Naturally it is better to use acceptable, stereotyped terms. . . .
> This is the very essence of metaphor. . . . If I ask for a 'mild'
> cigarette or a 'beautiful' car, while I can't define these
> attributes literally, I still know that they indicate something
> desirable. . . . The average motorist isn't sure at all what
> 'octane' in gasoline actually is. . . . But he does know vaguely
> that it is something good. So he orders 'high-octane' gasoline,
> because he desires this essence quality behind the meaningless
> surface jargon.[53]

53. Ibid., p. 100.

In other words, no sooner has the discourse of advertising awakened desire than it subjects it to generalization of the vaguest kind. Reduced to their simplest expression, the deep motives are keyed to a ready-instituted code of connotations, and 'choice', fundamentally, can only seal the collusion between this *moral* order and the individual's deepest wishes. Such is the alchemy of the 'psychological label'.[54]

In actuality, this stereotyped calling-forth of deep motives is nothing but a form of *censorship*. The ideology of personal fulfilment and the triumphant illogicality of drives supposedly freed from guilt are in fact merely a tremendous effort to materialize the superego. *What is 'personalized' in the object is primarily censorship.* No matter how much the philosophers of consumption may revel in the notion of deep motives as potentials for immediate happiness which have merely to be freed, the fact remains that the unconscious is conflicted, and inasmuch as advertising mobilizes it, it mobilizes it *as* conflict. Advertising does not liberate drives; first and foremost it liberates phantasies that serve to inhibit those drives. Hence the ambiguity of the object, in which the individual finds no route to self-transcendence, but merely an ambiguous retreat simultaneously to his desires and to the forces that censor those desires. We thus once more encounter the overall pattern of gratification/frustration described above: with its purely formal reduction of tensions and its ever-vain regressions, what the object invariably ensures is a perpetual renewal of conflicts. Here, perhaps, is a definition of the form of alienation particular to our time: our internal conflicts or 'deep tendencies' are mobilized and alienated in the process of consumption, in exactly the same way as labour-power is alienated in the process of production.

54. Comparing advertising to a kind of *magic* is really giving it too much credit, however. The nominalist lexicon of the alchemists has something of a genuine language about it, structured as it is by a praxis of research and interpretation. By contrast, the nominalism of 'brands' is strictly immanent – and congealed by economic imperatives.

Nothing has really changed – it is just that strictures on self-fulfilment are here no longer imposed by means of oppressive laws or norms of obedience; repression is ensured instead through 'free' actions (buying, choosing, consuming), through spontaneous cathexes, through a sort of internalization operating within gratification itself.

A Universal Code: Status

The objects-cum-advertising system therefore constitutes less a language, whose living syntax it lacks, than a set of significations. Impoverished yet efficient, it is basically a code. It does not structure the personality, but designates and classifies it. It does not structure social relationships, but breaks them down into a hierarchical repertoire. In its formal expression it constitutes a universal system for the identification of social rank: the code of 'status'.

In the context of 'consumer society', the notion of rank as a yardstick of social being tends to assume the simplified form of 'status'. Status in this sense is still measured in terms of power, authority and responsibility, yet fundamentally the message now is 'There is no responsibility without a Lip watch!' Advertising always refers explicitly to the object as to the essential criterion: 'You will be judged by such and such', 'The elegant woman is recognizable by such and such', and so on. No doubt objects have always played an identifying role of this kind, but formerly they did so in parallel – and this often in a purely auxiliary way – with other systems: gestural, ritual or ceremonial systems, language, rank at birth, codes of moral values, etc. The peculiarity of our own society is that all such other means of gauging rank are gradually giving way to the code of 'status'. Naturally this code applies in varying degrees according to socio-economic level, but the social function of advertising is to bring everyone under its sway. It is a moral code, for it is sanctioned by the group, and any infraction of it entails the apportionment of some measure of guilt. It is a totalitarian code, for no one escapes it; escaping it in a private sense cannot prevent us from participating every day in its collective development. Not believing in it still means believing sufficiently in other people's belief in it to adopt a sceptical stance. Even actions intended as resistance to it must be defined in terms of a society that conforms to it.

Nor is this code without its positive aspects. In the first place, it is no more arbitrary than any other code. After all, even in our own eyes, value resides in the car that we change every year, in the part of town where we live, and in the multitude of objects with which we surround ourselves and which distinguish us from other people. True, that is not the whole story, but have not codes of value always been partial and arbitrary (and moral codes more than any)?

Secondly, the code of 'status' does constitute a socialization, and a total secularization, of distinguishing signs, and consequently contributes to the emancipation – at least in the formal sense – of social relations. Not only do objects make material life more tolerable by proliferating as commodities, they likewise make the relative standing of people more tolerable by gaining general acceptance as identifying signs. One thing may be said in favour of the 'status' system: it has the virtue of rendering obsolete all the old rituals of caste or class, along – in a general way – with all preceding (and preclusive) criteria of social discrimination.

Thirdly, this code offers a *universal* system of decipherable signs for the first time in history. Perhaps it is to be regretted that it is usurping the place of all other codes, but it is arguable, conversely, that the gradual exhaustion of other systems (birth, class, function), the widening of competition, a greater social mobility, the accelerating fissiparity of social groups and the growing instability and proliferation of languages all created the necessity for a code which, by virtue of its straightforward universality, could guarantee clear and unencumbered communication. In a world where millions of men and women pass one another every day without being acquainted, the code of 'status' fulfils an essential social function by addressing people's vital need for knowledge of others. The fact is, however, that this universalization and this effectiveness are achieved only at the cost of a radical simplification, an impoverishment and a well-nigh definitive regression of the 'language' of value: 'Individuals define themselves through their objects.' Coherence is achieved through the institution of a combinatorial system or repertoire – a language that is functional, certainly, but symbolically and structurally immiserated.

What is more, the fact that a system of identification is now in place which is clearly legible to all, that the signs of value are entirely socialized and objectivized, by no means implies any true 'democratization'. On the contrary, it would appear that *the insistence on univocal reference merely exacerbates the desire to discriminate*: within the very framework of this homogeneous system, a perpetually renewed obsession with hierarchies and distinctions is to be observed. Even though barriers of morality, social convention and language have been overturned, new barriers and exclusions have arisen in the realm of objects: a new class or caste morality is thus enabled to colonize the most material and hitherto unchallengeable of spheres.

So, while the code of 'status' is at present coming to constitute a universal apparatus of signification that is immediately readable, facilitating the free flow of social representations from one end of society to the other, this does not mean that society is becoming more transparent. The code produces an illusion of transparency, an illusion of readable social relations, behind which the real structure of production and real social relationships remain illegible. A society would be transparent only if knowledge of the apparatus of signification was *simultaneously* knowledge of social structures and social realities. This is not so in the case of the objects-cum-advertising system, which offers nothing but a code of meaning that is always complicitous and always opaque. What is more, though it may provide a formal security thanks to its coherence, this code is also the best means for the global social order to extend its immanent and permanent rule to all individuals.

Conclusion:
towards a definition of 'consumption'

I should like to conclude this discussion of the various levels of the relationship to objects as an operative system with some attempt to define 'consumption'. It is to consumption, after all, that all aspects of practice in this area tend at present to lead.

Just so long as it is freed once and for all from its current meaning, that of a mechanism for satisfying needs, consumption may indeed be deemed a defining mode of our industrial civilization. For consumption is surely *not* that passive process of absorption and appropriation which is contrasted to the supposedly active mode of production, thus counterposing two oversimplified patterns of behaviour (and of alienation). It has to be made clear from the outset that consumption is an active form of relationship (not only to objects, but also to society and to the world), a mode of systematic activity and global response which founds our entire cultural system.

It has to be made clear that objects and material goods are not in fact the object of consumption – they are the object merely of needs and of the satisfaction of needs. From time immemorial people have bought, possessed, enjoyed and spent, but this does not mean that they were 'consuming'. The festivals of 'primitive' peoples, the largesse of the feudal lord, the luxury of the nineteenth-century bourgeois – none of these amounted to consumption. And if we are justified in using this term to describe present-day society, it is not because we now eat more or better, not because we absorb more images and messages, and not because we have more appliances and gadgets at our disposal. Neither the volume of goods nor the satisfaction of needs serves properly to define the notion of consumption, for these are simply the preconditions of consumption.

Consumption is not a material practice, nor is it a phenomenology of 'affluence'. It is not defined by the nourishment we take in, nor by the clothes we clothe ourselves with, nor by the car we use, nor by the oral and visual matter of the images and messages we receive. It is defined, rather, by the organization of all these things into a signifying fabric: consumption is *the virtual totality of all objects and messages ready-constituted as a more or less coherent discourse*. If it has any meaning at all, consumption means *an activity consisting of the systematic manipulation of signs*.

Traditional symbolic objects (tools, furniture, the house itself) were the mediators of a real relationship or a directly experienced situation, and their substance and form bore the clear imprint of the conscious or unconscious dynamic of that relationship. They were thus *not arbitrary*. Although they were bound by connotations – pregnant, freighted with connotations – they remained living objects on account of their inward and transitive orientation with respect to human actions, whether collective or individual. Such objects are not consumed. *To become an object of consumption, an object must first become a sign.* That is to say: it must become external, in a sense, to a relationship that it now merely signifies. It is thus *arbitrary* – and not inconsistent with that concrete relationship: it derives its consistency, and hence its meaning, from an abstract and systematic relationship to all other sign-objects. Only in this context can it be 'personalized', can it become part of a series, and so on; only thus can it be consumed, never in its materiality, but in its *difference*.

This conversion of the object to the systematic status of a sign implies the simultaneous transformation of the human relationship into a relationship of consumption – of consuming and being consumed. In and through objects this relationship is at once consummated and abolished;[1] the object becomes its inescapable mediation – and, before long, the sign that replaces it altogether.

So what is consummated and consumed is never the object but the relationship itself, signified yet absent, simultaneously included and excluded; it is the *idea of the relationship* that is consumed in the series of objects that displays it.

The relationship is no longer directly experienced: it has become abstract, been abolished, been transformed into a sign-object, and thus consumed.

This status of the relationship/object is governed at every level by the imperatives of production. The whole apparatus of advertising suggests that the living relationship, with its contradictions, must not be allowed to disturb the 'rational' order of production, and that it should be consumed like everything else. It must be 'personalized' so that it can be incorporated into the system. Here we rediscover, in its most extreme expression, the formal logic of the commodity as analysed by Marx: just as needs, feelings, culture, knowledge – in short, all the properly human faculties – are integrated as commodities into the order of production, and take on material form as productive forces so that they can be sold, so likewise all desires, projects and demands, all passions and all relationships, are now abstracted (or materialized) as signs and as objects to be bought and consumed. Take the couple, for example, whose objective *raison d'être* is now the consumption of objects – including the objects that formerly symbolized the relationship.[2]

1. [*Translator's note*: The author here and in the ensuing discussion exploits the fact that French has only one word (*consommer*) for both 'consume' and 'consummate'. I have therefore been obliged to use the two English words, or to paraphrase, in order to retain all the resonances of the text.]
2. In the United States married couples have even been encouraged to get new wedding rings every year, and to make their relationship 'meaningful' by buying gifts 'together'.

The beginning of Georges Perec's novel *Les choses* is instructive in this context:

> The eye, at first, would glide over the gray rug of a long corridor, high and narrow. The wall would be cabinets, whose copper fittings would gleam. Three engravings . . . would lead to a leather curtain, hanging from large rings of black-veined wood, that a simple gesture would suffice to slide back. . . . It would be a living room, about twenty-one feet long and nine feet wide. On the left, in a sort of alcove, a large couch of worn black leather would be flanked by two book cases in pale wild-cherry wood, on which books would be piled helter-skelter. Above the divan a nautical chart would run the whole length of the wall panel. Beyond a little low table, under a silk prayer rug attached to the wall with three copper nails with large heads, and balancing the leather hanging, another divan, perpendicular to the first, upholstered in light brown velvet, would lead to a small piece of furniture on high legs, lacquered in dark red, with three shelves that would hold bric-à-brac; agates and stone eggs, snuffboxes, jade ashtrays. . . . Farther on . . . small boxes and records, next to a closed phonograph of which only four machine-turned steel knobs would be visible. . . . [3]

Despite the thick mellow nostalgia that envelops this 'interior', it is clear that nothing in it has the slightest symbolic value any longer. One need only compare this description with any description of an interior by Balzac to see that no human relationship has left its imprint on these things: everything in Perec's décor is a sign, and purely a sign. Nothing has presence, nothing has a history – even though everything is laden with references: Oriental, Scottish,

3. Georges Perec, *Les choses, une histoire des années soixante* (Paris: Julliard, 1965), p. 12 [English translation by Helen R. Lane: *Things: A Story of the Sixties* (New York: Grove Press, 1967), pp. 11–12].

Early American, etc. The *only thing* all these objects have is their uniqueness: they are abstract in their difference, which is their mode of referentiality, and enter into combination with one another precisely by virtue of that abstractness. We are indubitably in the realm of consumption.[4]

As Perec's novel continues, we get a sense of how a system of sign-objects of this kind functions: far from symbolizing the relationship, what these objects actually describe, from the externality of their continual 'referring', is the relationship's emptiness, which is discernible at every moment in the lack of existence that each of the partners has for the other. Jérôme and Sylvie do not exist as a couple: their sole reality is as 'Jérôme-and-Sylvie' – as a pure complicity surfacing within the system of objects that signifies it. Nor can it be said that objects are an automatic substitute for the relationship that is lacking, that they serve to fill a void: on the contrary, they *describe* this void, the locus of the relationship, pursuant to a process which is a way of not living the relationship while at the same time (save in cases of complete regression) exposing it to the light of the possibility of its being lived. Thus the relationship is not sucked into the absolute positivity of objects but articulated with those objects as with so many solid points in a chain of signifiers – except that here the signifying configuration of objects is usually impoverished, schematic and closed, and deals only with the *idea* of a relationship, not with a relationship that can be lived. Leather couch, phonograph, bric-à-brac, jade ashtrays: it is *the idea of the relationship* that is signified in these objects, that is 'consumed' in them and hence abolished as anything to be directly experienced.

This implies that consumption may be defined as a *total idealist practice* of a systematic kind which goes way beyond relations to

4. In the Perec 'interior' we are dealing with objects made transcendent by fashion, not with the 'serial' objects of mass production. Total cultural constraint – cultural terrorism – reigns here. But this makes no difference to the system of consumption itself.

objects and interpersonal relations and extends to every level of history, communication and culture. Thus the demand for culture is a living demand, but it is only the *idea* of the collector's edition or the colour lithograph in the dining-room that is actually consumed. The demand for revolution is likewise a living demand, but so long as it is not actualized in practice it will be consumed as the idea of Revolution. As an idea the Revolution is indeed eternal, and must needs remain eternally consumable just like any other idea – all ideas, even the most contradictory, being capable of coexistence as signs in the idealist logic of consumption. The Revolution is therefore signified by a combinatorial terminology, a vocabulary of unmediated terms, in which it appears as already realized – and by which it is indeed 'consumed'.[5]

Similarly, objects of consumption constitute an idealist lexicon of signs wherein the will to live itself is discernible in an ever-receding materiality. Once again Perec's book makes the point:

> It sometimes seemed to them that a whole life could go harmoniously by between these book-lined walls, among these objects so perfectly domesticated that the two of them would end up believing that they had been forever created for their own use alone. . . . But they would not feel themselves tied down by them; on certain days they would go looking for adventure. Nothing they planned would be impossible.[6]

5. Consumed, that is, and at the same time consummated – hence also destroyed. To say that the revolution is consumed/consummated in the idea of the Revolution means that the revolution is both fulfilled (formally) and abolished in that idea; and what is presented as already realized is thenceforward consumable in an unmediated manner. [*Translator's note*: On 'consume'/'consummate', see note 1 above.]
6. *Les choses*, French edition, p. 15 [English trans., pp. 15–16].

But note the conditional in this last sentence – and indeed, the novel goes on to give this prediction the lie: there are no more projects – only objects. Not that the project has disappeared, exactly: it is just that its 'realization' as a sign embodied in the object is taken as satisfaction enough. The object of consumption is thus the precise form of the project's self-renunciation.

This explains why THERE ARE NO LIMITS TO CONSUMPTION. If consumption were indeed what it is naïvely assumed to be, namely a process of absorption or devouring, a saturation point would inevitably be reached. If consumption were indeed tied to the realm of needs, some sort of progress towards satisfaction would presumably occur. We know very well, however, that nothing of the kind happens: people simply want to consume more and more. This compulsion is attributable neither to some psychological determinism ('once a drunk always a drunk', and so forth) nor to the pressure of some simple desire for prestige. That consumption seems irrepressible is due, rather, to the fact that it is indeed a total idealist practice which no longer has anything to do (beyond a certain threshold) either with the satisfaction of needs or with the reality principle. Its dynamism derives from the ever-disappointed project now implicit in objects. Thus embedded in unmediated form in the object, the project transfers its existential dynamic to the systematic and limitless acquisition of consumption's sign-objects. This means that consumption must henceforward either keep surpassing itself or keep repeating itself merely in order to remain what it is – namely, a reason for living. The very will to live, fragmented, disappointed, signified, is condemned to repeat itself and repeatedly abolish itself in a succession of objects. In this context all attempts to 'moderate' consumption or to devise a grid of needs capable of normalizing it attest to nothing but a naïve or grotesque moralism.

The systematic and limitless process of consumption arises from the disappointed demand for totality that underlies the project of life. In their ideality sign-objects are all equivalent and may multiply infinitely; indeed, they *must multiply* in order at every moment to make up for a reality that is absent. Consumption is irrepressible, in the last reckoning, because it is founded upon a *lack*.

AVAILABLE IN THE RADICAL THINKERS SERIES

Minima Moralia:
Reflections on a
Damaged Life
THEODOR ADORNO

Paperback 1 84467 051 1
$12/£6/$14CAN
256 pages • 5 x 7.75 inches

For Marx
LOUIS ALTHUSSER

Paperback 1 84467 052 X
$12/£6/$14CAN
272 pages • 5 x 7.75 inches

The System of Objects
JEAN BAUDRILLARD

Paperback 1 84467 053 8
$12/£6/$14CAN
224 pages • 5 x 7.75 inches

Liberalism and Democracy
NORBERTO BOBBIO

Paperback 1 84467 062 7
$12/£6/$14CAN
112 pages • 5 x 7.75 inches

AVAILABLE IN THE RADICAL THINKERS SERIES

The Politics of Friendship
JACQUES DERRIDA

Paperback 1 84467 054 6
$12/£6/$14CAN
320 pages • 5 x 7.75 inches

The Function of Criticism
TERRY EAGLETON

Paperback 1 84467 055 4
$12/£6/$14CAN
136 pages • 5 x 7.75 inches

Signs Taken for Wonders:
On the Sociology of Literary
Forms

FRANCO MORETTI

Paperback 1 84467 056 2
$12/£6/$14CAN
288 pages • 5 x 7.75 inches

The Return of the Political
CHANTAL MOUFFE

Paperback 1 84467 057 0
$12/£6/$14CAN
176 pages • 5 x 7.75 inches

AVAILABLE IN THE RADICAL THINKERS SERIES